The Way
to
Communicate

The Way
to
Communicate

Michael W. Harkins

Portsmouth Publishing
Berkeley 2010

Portsmouth Publishing
Berkeley, California
www.portsmouthpublishing.com

www.thewaytocommunicate.com

ISBN-13: 978-0-9798757-2-4
ISBN-10: 0-9798757-2-2

Printed in the United States of America

Cover and book design by Writesite
www.writesite.com

To Elizabeth
You are my world

Contents

Introduction

You talkin' to me?

In our connected world of multiple methods and avenues of communication, legions of people have difficulty communicating with someone standing right in front of them.

Many otherwise capable people struggle to establish a comfortable, effective dialog with an audience, whether that audience is a project team at work, a promotions board, a national sales meeting, a social networking event, or a colleague during an intimate but important conversation.

Effective, dynamic presenters, public speakers, and entertainers know that personal connection is the highest priority in any conversation, presentation or performance. Without personal connection, no one cares, no one listens, and no one watches. Whether you want to communicate to the person sitting across from you, or to one-thousand people in an auditorium, you have to connect to them. You have to connect. Even in a filled auditorium, you still need to make it seem as if you are having a one-on-one conversation with each person in the audience.

The ability to communicate with someone, to connect with them, to convince them that "I do, truly, understand, I do, truly, care," is fundamental to helping people grow, learn, choose, and act. Few messages in life are as important as the one that conveys, "I care."

Everything we do – how we interact with people, how we stand, how we look, what we say, how we say it, and how we listen – communicates something about us at every moment.

1

The Way to Communicate teaches how to tap into our core and build upon our inherent sense of humanity, empathy, and self-awareness to become a better communicator. Rising from this basic, philosophical foundation, The Way to Communicate then provides the mental, physical, technical and practical tools that enable anyone to markedly improve personal communication skills and effectively communicate any message to anyone, from a one-on-one conversation to a presentation in front of a packed auditorium.

Got a message to communicate? Me too.

We are a sense-oriented species, driven largely by sight and sound, drawn to messages at every instant of our lives. We consciously and sub-consciously select, from tens-of-thousands, the sights and sounds which receive our immediate attention, and those which are relegated to short- or long-term storage, or deletion. I will sift through, or sit through, a poorly organized, poorly presented message if its subject is of intense interest to me. I may do the same if the subject is of moderate interest. But, I may dismiss a message before its importance becomes clear if its presentation is sloppy, confusing, or disrespectful.

Whether I'm a listener in an intimate conversation or sitting amidst a sea of people in an auditorium, I need to feel a personal connection with the speaker. I have to care. Empathy, respect, and connection form the foundation of effective, personal communication; the presenter must evoke those attributes and the listener must feel them.

Are they the elements of your foundation?

Communication should not be confused with the tools or platforms of communication. Sound systems, projectors, charts, DVDs, Flash animations, YouTube videos, Twitter, blogs, org charts and memos are the tools of communication, but they do not communicate.

Presented as a definition, effective personal communication requires more than a sender and receiver, and more than a conveyance of information – it requires delivering information in context and in a manner that conveys the information with an easily discernable, emotional component.

Take that definition and word it in a more pragmatic, everyday manner and it simply means I've got something I want to let you know about and you're willing to listen.

We communicate when we connect, and we can only connect if we empathize. When I evoke and recognize within myself those personal attributes I share with you, I can connect with you. When you accept my concerns, when you empathize with me, you accept my sincerity, my truth, and then I truly communicate with you. When I speak the truth and believe in my own purpose, with no agenda other than sharing my truth, I will connect with you.

But, if I am a skillful presenter of a manufactured truth, if my agenda is to have you believe, even as I do not believe, I will only connect with some of you. And at some point, many that I do connect with will discern that I am but the shine on the surface of a shallow pool.

Communication is connection, connection is empathy, and empathy is truth. Great communicating is the conveyance of truth.

We all have to do it, but only YOU can do it

PowerPoint slides don't connect; video, animation or elaborate staging don't connect; pretty pictures and in-your-face graphics, they won't connect either. Any of those may evoke a reaction, cause a stir, get people interested or fired up or laughing or crying or yelling or falling asleep, but in the end it's a person-to-person world. You have to connect to people to communicate effectively. Communicating is about more than the message, it's about conveying the emotion, the feeling of what's being communicated.

A communicator wants to plug-in to an audience, send energy and get energy in return. Great presenters, motivational speakers, and stand-up comedians all make an effort to connect to their audience. It may start with only one person: the comedian points to someone in the audience and asks a direct question, or, as a dynamic presenter reaches a dramatic, poignant statement in her speech, she makes and holds eye contact with someone. That single connection is seen and felt by the audience, then spreads through the audience on a wave of empathy and humanity.

"Ah," they think, "yeah, yeah, that's right."

Connection, engagement, call it what you feel comfortable calling it, but it's the basis for real communication.

I am...

I am a respected media and communications consultant. I am a communicator, but I am not a certified expert in communication. I do not have a Ph.D. or any other degree in communication studies. I left college in my second year to go on the road with a band.

I have talents which contribute to my communication skills, but talent, which I define as an understanding of and aptitude for something without benefit of training, is only a foundation. I have spent my entire adult life building on my foundation. By learning, improving, and exploring every nuance of professional creativity and communications, I have built a career designing, writing, producing, presenting and teaching communication.

Diversity builds character...or something like that

I kicked around for a year after high school, until a very low draft number prompted me to join the Army. I spent a little over three years jumping out of airplanes. I took some art school correspondence classes during that time, and I began to write. I came out of the Army, enrolled in art school full time, acted in some community theatre plays, did freelance art jobs, and landed my first paid acting gig: I was Clarence K. Watts, the electric man, part of a five-man sideshow troupe for a summer at Marriott's Great America. We entertained people as they waited to attend the park's circus show (four performances a day, sometimes to a crowd of a thousand, six days a week).

In late 1976, I stumbled into the 'real' music industry, as opposed to the 'local' music industry scene...which means I stopped playing in local clubs with local bands and began working as a roadie with a band that had a recording contract. I spent a decade in the touring and concert video industry, followed by years of freelance and consulting projects, everything from writing and

4

shooting corporate videos, to medical illustration, to writing magazine articles. I also kept my acting chops by dubbing dialog for a couple of films.

As I enhanced and refined my skills, I began a long period of corporate and business work. I now have three decades of experience working for individuals and organizations ranging from Michael Jackson to Wells Fargo Bank, Gatorade to Schwinn, and the American Red Cross to the Wild Horse Sanctuary of Shingletown, California (the country's first wild mustang sanctuary). While I brought my own knowledge and experience to every assignment, I took away invaluable insights as to how communications do and don't work at the highest, pressure-driven, professional levels. These experiences have given me the many tools and insights to create much of the Way to Communicate's method, while a lifelong interest in the martial arts and Zen form much of the method's underlying philosophy.

I worked side-by-side with, and was heavily influenced by, world class entertainers, powerful CEOs, senior executives, and business owners. Their range of communication skills varied, but I always absorbed something from them that I could apply to myself. I shared these insights as I began to coach others in the ways of communication.

The best communicators have always been those I believed. This is not as simplistic as it reads.

Media and communications professionals, especially those who work directly with actors and spokespeople, quickly recognize someone who is inherently sincere in front of a live audience, and someone who is all shine and no structure. I've come in contact with and observed speakers who were naturally gifted storytellers, with great focus, concentration, and control of the audience. I've also worked with people so full of themselves they were dismissive of objective input that would have vastly improved their effectiveness.

Somewhere in the middle are the majority of communicators, sincere but untrained, who work diligently to connect with their audience.

Connecting is the challenge no matter who you are or what

you do. Surprisingly, many challenges to effectively communicating are the same, whether on the macro scale of a Fortune 500 company or the micro scale of manager-to-employee conversation.

I've witnessed the best and worst of it. While the technical and stylistic challenges to communicating effectively are many and diverse, the most important attribute of communicating effectively is often overlooked: it's a person-to-person world. YouTube videos, Facebook pages, blogs, presentations, brochures, great clothes, attractiveness, all of these can have some bearing on whether we like someone, buy the product, or accept the offer. But the important choices we make in our lives are universally driven by interactions with another person.

The scale of a presentation, discussion, or conversation may be great – how to position the company for an IPO – or intimate – accept or reject the job offer – but no matter who's talking about what, at any level, it's still a person-to-person world.

And so, from me to you, I give you this

We're all capable of communicating, but some of us get in our own way. We hide behind laptops and projectors, use podiums as shields, make inappropriate jokes, or, for all our sincerity and hard work, we've just never learned how to communicate correctly.

It's time to change that lack of awareness and become a better, relaxed, effective communicator. The world needs great communicators, and I want to help you become one. It is possible to feel as comfortable in front of any sized crowd as it is during a conversation with a friend. It's a moment that you can reach, and when that moment happens, you will no longer be presenting, because you will have integrated the Way's skills and techniques, made them your own, and you will simply be you.

Providing the path to "simply being you" in front of any audience is the ultimate goal of The Way to Communicate.

The Way to Communicate integrates techniques and insights from creative writing, martial arts, meditation, physical fitness, acting and stage performance. This may seem initially to be a mash-up of barely relatable sources, but they have common traits

6

and philosophies that when understood and placed into practice, enhance your effectiveness as a communicator, and positively affect many other aspects of your life.

The Sections – Rehearsal, Run Thru, Performance

The Way to Communicate concentrates on three aspects of you as a person to develop you as a communicator. These areas, the Mind, Body, and Stage, and their relationships to becoming a better communicator, are explored in the book's three sections.

In sections one and two, Rehearsal and Run Thru, you discover and develop personal attributes within the Mind and Body areas. In the final section, Performance, we lead you to and through communication scenarios. This progression – foundational elements, each element's attributes, and the integration of everything into a final scenario, is analogous to learning the basics of dance, combining those basics into extended dance movements, then integrating all the movements into a routine.

Section One - Rehearsal

In Rehearsal you become aware of common emotional and physical attributes – breathing, moving, observing – that sustain your very existence, explore just how unaware you can be of these attributes, and discover how that unawareness affects anyone's ability to communicate.

Section Two – Run Thru

The exercises, techniques, and guidance in Run Thru develop your comfort level as a communicator by building upon your new levels of awareness and using them daily, from getting dressed in the morning through to the end of the work day.

Section Three - Performance

Finally, in Performance, we walk from the wings to the podium, guiding you through every aspect of preparation and delivery of a presentation, speech, or participation in an interview or social situation.

The Attributes

Here are individual attributes of Mind, Body, and Stage, that when integrated into our everyday lives create connections to others and enhance our ability to communicate. In sections one and two, you are introduced to and develop these attributes:

Mind - awareness, clarity, focus, vision

Body - awareness, balance, breath, flexibility

In the final section, your Mind and Body attributes join with your Stage attributes to create your enhanced communication abilities:

Stage - awareness, content, empathy, focus

Development of the Mind and Body attributes throughout sections one and two prepares you for the using the more advanced Stage attributes in the last section, Performance, the place and time where everything comes together as your personal method of presentation – your optimal moment of communication. The Stage attributes come into play in any presentation environment: a one-on-one sales meeting, working a trade show booth, or presenting at an all-employee meeting.

The Performance section includes expanded guidance on several specific aspects of communicating:

Be Normal is an explanation of how and why to prepare, and how not to prepare, for an appearance or presentation.

The Switch reveals how to create and commit to a cue that places you in Performance mode. Once you turn on your Switch, you place yourself in heightened awareness and stay there until you have finished your presentation or appearance.

The Audience is about connecting to and working with sometimes friendly, sometimes not-so friendly people of an audience. Sometimes you're sure you've connected, other times it feels as if you're speaking English and your audience only understands Martian. This advice and guidance enlightens you as to why the otherwise lovely woman who appears to be growling at you may not be having a bad time at all.

Be True is my life-guiding mantra. To Be True is to have no agenda other than your goal, where there is no underlying, hidden or deceptive reason for your actions. At its core, the Be True philosophy is to do everything for the right reason, all the time. Here's an example:

During a frank and open conversation with a commercially successful, highly regarded musician, he stated that commercial success didn't matter to him. Yes, it made life somewhat easier, and it was fun in many ways, but he would have been as happy playing in a polka band if he had to, and he was 'being true'.

He had always played to play, and had never played with the goal of becoming a wealthy entertainer. That's being true.

As you develop your newfound awareness and communication skills, your ability to connect with an audience will continually improve, until you reach a level of comfort that is beyond presenting, beyond performing, and where you are simply being 'you'.

There is something in this book for everyone who wishes to improve their communication skills. You shouldn't, however, expect to absorb all the information, utilize all the guidance, or execute all the techniques immediately.

If you have never felt comfortable presenting or speaking in front of an audience, feel varying degrees of nervousness or anxiety, or are about to embark upon a career or situation that requires presenting on a regular basis, I recommend reading from the beginning of the book.

If you're confident in your communication abilities, but want to refine your skills and discover new insights, you can begin with section two, Run Thru, or section three, Performance. I do recommend reading section one, if only to possibly discover something new about yourself or about the way you communicate.

However and to what degree you embrace The Way to Communicate, MAKE THIS BOOK YOUR OWN. Write in it, fold pages, circle passages, underline and do whatever is necessary to easily locate and reinforce anything that really resonates for you and keeps the attributes of an effective communicator a mere page-flip away.

Section One - Rehearsal
Before We Begin, Let's Go Over How to Begin

Your beginning is a beginning, your first step is a first step

We begin by pondering something which may not seem relevant to presenting or communicating. We begin with a short description of a judo lesson.

My first judo lesson, more than forty-five years ago, was no different than every first judo lesson ever taught and every future first judo lesson: an explanation of why a student bows before he or she steps onto the mat; a physical warm-up; how to stand and why; and how to fall and why.

There were no throws – as thrower or thrown – and no sparring for almost the entire hour. While you may not have any knowledge about judo, the core aspects of my first judo lesson should be familiar, because it's how we learn anything, from checkers to computer programming. No touchdown pass is thrown before knowing how to properly grip the ball; no soccer ball bends like Beckham's before mastering the dribble and pass; and no baseball makes it over the fence unless a batter knows how to stand in the box, and hold and swing the bat.

It is a basic concept for everything, in life, education, and sports. It seems, however, to have been overlooked by a majority of communicators. Presenters who have rudimentary or advanced PowerPoint or Keynote skills, doing a presentation for the third or the thirty-third time, may have never been exposed to presentation or public speaking training.

People who have to present or provide information to a group may have come into their current job right out of college, or may be veterans in their industry, and may be comfortable 'enough' presenting or speaking to groups of people; they continue putting six or seven bullet points on each electronic slide, include some clip art, and read their slides aloud to their captive audiences; or they hold meetings that their teams have come to dread...

...and they've never taken a public-speaking class.

Huh. How about that?

Outside, we use a computer and a projector, or pen and paper, maybe just one or the other; inside, we use everything, all the time.

A human being is a living example of an interconnected system. We can't perform any one function without bringing other functions into play: thoughts and actions arise from brain activity; the brain requires oxygenated-blood to function; oxygenated-blood requires oxygen delivered via the lungs. The whole process is wondrously complicated.

Tense up, take short, hyper-ventilating breaths, let the adrenaline have its way, and brain function is affected. That's stage fright, which many of you may experience while speaking or presenting, even though you may never have been on an 'actual' stage.

The more fit we are, physically and mentally, the better we physically and mentally perform. The physical fitness connection to intellectual performance is not a recent notion; medical studies validate that being physically fit positively affects the intellectual process. Highly-functional professionals understand that thinking clearly, and the ability to put in long, grueling work hours is directly related to overall health and fitness levels.

Studies also prove what we know instinctively, that the more relaxed we are, the easier it is to do anything. The clearest example of actually seeing relaxation's relationship to peak physical performance is slow-motion replay of athletes in competition. Visualize the frantic flow of energy and physical banging that goes on during an intense basketball game. Suddenly, a player elevates out of the chaos, seems to float for a moment, then releases a high, arcing shot that spins through the air and into the basket. The level of relaxation within an otherwise chaotic environment is clearly evident.

Another visual example of a heightened state of relaxation and focus are the slow-motion replays of world-class sprinters, so relaxed at their optimal performance levels that the skin and muscles of their faces flop around noticeably.

Athletes know they can't do their best if they're tense; they don't hold their breath; they breathe, they relax. That's an important lesson for all of us.

Awareness

Great athletes, performers, and leaders all share an important attribute: they have great awareness.

A focused, relaxed mind is very important in any endeavor, not just in the arena of athletics. The ability to focus, to clear out distractions, keep them at bay and be totally present and attuned to the surroundings, these are attributes of awareness possessed by great achievers in any field. In all endeavors -- actors, athletes, pilots, surgeons, police officers -- significant time and effort are spent on focused, relaxed concentration and awareness training.

From organizing to decision making, spur of the moment negotiating to methodical project planning, or spinning down your own mental hard drive so you can simply relax and enjoy the moment, mental fitness shares the same attributes as physical fitness: mental fitness and awareness are required to act or respond in a fluid, appropriate manner, to known, expected, or spontaneous stimuli.

To achieve any level of mental fitness and agility, you have to be aware. Awareness is the anchor component of The Way to Communicate; it is an important attribute of the Mind, Body, and Stage elements.

Are you really aware? When you look around, do you see, or do you just look?

Even successful, highly-functional types, who should have the ability to be effective, riveting communicators, may fall short because they fail to have a basic physical and mental awareness of the environment and, more importantly, of themselves, as they speak. Many presenters are so focused on the presentation itself that they have no self-awareness at all. Whether a presenter is overly focused on getting through the presentation, or un-focused due to something like stage fright, the lack of overall awareness manifests in many different ways, none of them helpful: poor posture; rapid, shallow breathing; not knowing where the glass of water is relative to the podium; fiddling with the remote to change the projected slide; and noticeably shifting and fidgeting, all of these are examples of elements that interfere with awareness, and the ability to effectively communicate.

And I haven't even mentioned the perils of not extending awareness to the audience, of not being aware of what's happening amidst the people with whom you are working so hard to connect.

Nothing starts when it starts, because everything starts before it starts. Be aware now, especially when now is the beginning.

Even though that Zen-like advice might be confusing initially, figuratively walk with me and I promise that at the end of this winding path we will arrive at a place of understanding, which is the place where you begin.

Everything starts at the beginning, yes, but the beginning isn't when you say "Good morning and thank you for this opportunity..." Your beginning is the idea, the job, or the assignment:

"Carol, you're going to deliver the first section of the presentation on our new product at the MegaTech conference."

Your beginning is your knowledge, your expertise, the data gathering, the outline, the graphics, the PowerPoint slides, the first seven drafts, the next four drafts, the travel logistics, the packing, travelling, the flight, the taxi ride, the hotel check-in...

Those are all beginnings, and you haven't even gotten to the show yet.

We begin with every moment

While most of us consider birth to be our personal 'beginning', others prefer the big, scientific perspective, wherein our beginning goes all the way back to the formation of the stars.

For our purposes, let's stay away from the galactic, existential view and agree on a more easily envisioned perspective.

And to do that, let's begin with a primer on drama and screenplays as a form of storytelling.

Yes, it is a winding path, but at least it's interesting.

Every moment in our lives is a scene from a three-act drama about life

At any given moment we're going somewhere, arriving somewhere, or leaving somewhere. We're planning to do something, doing something, or we've done something; that's our existence, and it's what we see as we watch a film (or any visual story medium).

Every three-act drama – the standard format for plays, TV shows and movies - is a series of events presented in a particular sequence. That may describe what a movie or TV show 'is', but the description lacks those elements that motivate us to give up our valuable time and become the drama's audience: the elements of love, laughter, tension, envy, empathy, sympathy, hate, jealousy, anger, justice, and on and on.

It is in the sharing of specific moments from characters' lives that stir within us our own emotions.

Individual film scenes vary from a few seconds to a few minutes (longer than three minutes is a rarity). There may be cuts, edits, and changes in point-of-view within a scene, but the scene itself is a self-contained unit, a snippet from a character's life. We watch a character rob a bank successfully, walk out of the bank, and the images dissolve to the next scene as he eats dinner, later, alone, in a small, neighborhood restaurant. We don't know what happened in the hour or two hours or six hours between when he left the bank and arrived to eat dinner at the restaurant.

Before this scene is over, we may find out what happened in the interim, by way of another character stopping by his table to talk, or by a cutaway shot to a TV reporter's story on a series of bank robberies that occurred throughout the afternoon. And, it may not actually matter what happened; the bank robber may have done all those mundane things that we real people do: showered, napped, read the paper, things like that.

Rest assured, though, as the screenwriter created the bank

robber's universe, the screenwriter certainly knows what happened in the time between the robbery and dinner. Whether seen for a few seconds crossing the street, or for three solid minutes reciting a soliloquy from Hamlet, every character is going somewhere, has come from somewhere, and is moving on to somewhere else. The writer's choices to show or not show what happened will, in the end, make the difference in how we feel about the story.

And our lives, as conceptualized for any story, are also a series of mini three-act dramas.

Characters have their beginnings chosen for them. You must become aware of and choose where you begin.

So, then, where is the beginning?

It's your choice, but choose wisely, because as you approach the podium or pick up your wireless controller, when you actually choose to begin greatly determines how you end, and how everyone feels about you and what you communicate.

Let's agree that by the time you begin your presentation, speech, or meeting, you will have started long before that particular beginning. And here is what you must accept before you begin: you must know your end before you know your beginning.

Back to the drama analogies, and let's bring in fiction and non-fiction books too.

Almost all screenwriters (and many novelists, but they are of a different breed for the sake of this discussion), know the end of their screenplays before typing the first words on page one. Knowing the end insures that everything in the screenplay, film, or play will always point to the end. This 'knowing' is important. At the conclusion, as the screen fades to black or as the curtain comes down, the audience may not accept the story's weaknesses, or places where credulity was stretched, but the majority will be satisfied if the story had a foundation of truth and logic for its twists and turns. Decisions, character choices and consequences, these can and will be discussed and debated, but the aggregate of the experience will hinge on everything in the story having conformed to logic and the natural laws of the universe.

Everything will have happened for a reason, and the reasons will have been decided and plotted so as to lead to the story's inevitable conclusion.

Read the above sentence again, because accepting it, understanding it and applying it is a big step upon the path of better communication. There is an old adage, "When you don't know where you're going, any road will get you there." If you're going to take me on a ride (your presentation, your report, your...), if I'm going to give you ten-minutes, forty-five minutes, an hour or a day of my valuable time, then I want to be assured that you know where you're going, and I want to feel that way from the first moment.

Therefore, your presentation's inevitable conclusion – the end of your speech, sales call or panel discussion – must be known to you long before your walk onto the stage.

What will they talk about as they leave?

We begin Rehearsal, the point of which is to make you aware of that which you are not aware, by asking a question you may believe is out of order: What will your audience talk about after?

What was the end you had in mind before you began?

Even though you haven't actually given your presentation yet (and even if you don't have one scheduled), you must decide what the audience will metaphorically take with them after your presentation. This decision – made now – guides everything to come.

Your inevitable conclusion is what you want your audience to talk about when they leave.

The premise is simple: always start from the end, because that way you'll always know where you're going, and you'll never be lost.

Everything you present points to your destination. It is a simple yet powerful, effective rule, and it can be applied to any communication and presentation project.

Athletes, whether it's baseball, football, basketball or soccer, are taught this same fundamental premise, even if they've never realized until now why they were doing it: follow-through. The follow-though of a propelled object is important for accuracy, and the accuracy of that end result -- the strike, the goal, splitting the uprights, hitting nothin' but net – is rooted in getting to the end of the motion correctly.

Know where you want it to go, concentrate on that end, and you succeed.

It doesn't mean that a presentation can't have some fun, some extra information, some data not specifically related to the reason for the presentation in the first place, but it does mean that if you do veer from your main points, you have to get back.

Always consider what your audience might say about you, about your message, because for all the valuable, enriching exercises and insights on these pages, this is a book about communicating, and a communicator's message must always be clear. You will be exposed to many anatomical, biological, creative, philosophical, and practical insights that contribute to your growth as a communicator, but I will constantly return to a very important question about communication: what are you communicating? The what is your end, and you must know your end before you begin.

You must know what you are communicating whether you're doing a presentation or a job interview.

In live drama, early rehearsals often include meetings to review and discuss what the play is about, its history, when and why it was written, and themes upon which it touches. Rehearsal begins by deciding what the play is truly about.

Your Rehearsal begins by deciding what your message is truly about.

The 'know your end' adage of screenwriters is the same concept actors use to construct the unseen lives of their characters, and for discovering how those characters arrive at the final destination. This process is called backstory, where writers and actors come to know the personal history of a character or story.

Whether you, your team or your department has been assigned to put together a PowerPoint presentation for a major industry conference, or you're scheduled to present orally to several senior executives, all communicating situations should start the same way, by answering the following questions:

What is your idea or mandate?
This is the follow-through, the destination, the inevitable

conclusion, what you want to get across to your audience, whether you want hundreds to walk out the room with this in their collective consciousness, or you want a new customer to reach for a pen and sign the contract the moment you finish your presentation.

What is the point you are making?

This is the refined, focused message. Your inevitable conclusion may be "we're the best, anywhere" but your point is based on what follows the word "because...", i.e., "we're the best anywhere, because we're the only company with true interstellar teleportation".

Who is the audience?

Peers? Strangers? Skeptics? Allies? Your content needs to match your audience, and so does your demeanor. Empathy and respect for your audience should always be foremost, and respect is about recognizing the capabilities and sensibilities of your audience. You wouldn't want to explain the how and why of 2+2=4 to a roomful of astrophysicists.

What and where is the venue?

Boardroom? Hotel suite? Panel discussion, a row of chairs open to the audience or a dais? Auditorium? Lunch or dinner at a restaurant? Have you been there before? The environment and where it is will be an important bubble into which you will insert yourself.

How are you making, the delivery?

Are you presenting on a stage? On the floor, level with your audience? Behind a podium? Can you walk around? Will you have projected slides? Will you be videotaped?

Answers to these questions point you to the end of your performance. The last two questions don't suggest that you must know every detail of how you will or won't move, or how you will or won't be able to see the audience, but they contribute to an overall awareness as you prepare.

Now that you understand that development of your presentation begins with the end, you can begin reverse engineering.

Yes, on that Zen path again, the signs now read, "if you want to go forward, you are best served by first going in reverse." For example:

"What do we require to present our software to these specific manufacturers?"

"What do we need to have so we can present our robust wine to this category of wine enthusiasts?"

"What materials and information will support my case for more money for the department and more new hires?"

Answers to these questions become the outlines and 'needs list' that is your presentation's foundation.

The mental, physical, and emotional aspects of becoming a better communicator are the focus of this book. Many of the elements and tasks for constructing a presentation, as I've reviewed above, are probably more familiar and comforting to many of you than is the thought of actually giving the presentation. I accept this, or I wouldn't be writing this book. Many writers will admit that the more enjoyable aspects of writing are not the writing itself but the researching and interviewing.

Many of you may be quite comfortable pulling together a presentation. This slight digression from how to improve your presenting skills is not that far of a digression at all, really. Just as the greatest actor has a difficult if not impossible task of mounting an acclaimed performance when the material is poorly written, you will have a very difficult time improving as a communicator if your presentation materials are poorly conceived.

I have developed and placed on The Way to Communicate website (www.thewaytocommunicate.com) what I call The Way of Presentation Development. Studying it will, in a very important way, contribute to your improvement as a presenter.

You are moving

You have accepted that while we are working on your personal presentation skills, you must know where you are going before you move forward to working on yourself.

You are on your way.

You've been to the website, downloaded The Way of Presentation Development (or it's on your schedule to do that); you're researching, writing, getting graphics and photos; if you're preparing for a sales call or interview, you're researching the business or company. We are in Rehearsal, the initial phase of improving your presentation skills.

Becoming aware of the whats and whys

During Rehearsal, we focus on making you aware of that which you are currently not aware.

The Way to Communicate's method, like our very existence, is based on the concept of an interconnected system, wherein everything works together, and a weakness in one area may severely hamper every other part of the system. Learning to use such a system, however, requires working first with each individual component.

Just as I had to learn how to stand and how to fall before I could attempt my first judo throw, you must learn, through exercises that focus on specific aspects of The Way to Communicate, those separate attributes that will eventually merge to make you a better communicator.

The learning process of anything is best undertaken when the mind is prepared to learn.

And Your Mind is where we start.

The Mind Attributes - awareness, clarity, focus, vision

Becoming aware

Biological and physiological processes are the 'how' of cotton mouth, lightheadedness, short-term memory loss, rapid heart rate, or excess perspiration. The why, however, as in "why do I start sweating like I'm in a sauna every time I have to stand in front of a group" and other similar, public speaking-oriented ponderings, are all variations of the same question: why does my mind let me down just when I need it most?

The range of answers to that and other "why" questions about public speaking anxiety is wide, but for those who suffer from it to any degree, and for those of you blessed with no nervousness, but desire to shore up your capabilities, we start with the mind.

The strategy to defeat the anxiety demons, or to enhance already established abilities, begins with making you aware of how to be aware.

Imagine suddenly realizing you're inside a dark box, no clue about day, time or location, then the box opens and you're all alone on a brightly-lit stage, with a large audience staring at you intently, quietly waiting for...something...

Speaker anxiety and stage fright can feel this way. A presenter dealing with this kind of situation may have been in the room for a minute or an hour, and it won't matter, because the perception of the situation – center stage in front of an expectant audience – is the same: a sudden inability to see anything clearly, breathe in a normal fashion, or have a coherent thought about the situation.

The reality of the moment is unchanged – a room, in a building, dozens of human beings seated in chairs, time moving in sixty-second increments – but the self-induced perceptions of everything around the presenter are created by the presenter's mind. It is the presenter's perception of the situation that needs adjustment.

For you students of The Way to Communicate, the adjustments to be made are your awareness of where you are, what you are doing, and of the realities of your situation's environment.

Your first exercise is to create an unbreakable habit.

From this point forward, any time you enter a space, look around and absorb the environment: the layout of the room, lighting, spacing of furniture; whether the room is warm or cold; do you hear piped in music; where are the windows; is there artwork on the walls; is the floor hard-surface or carpeted ?

Is the room noisy, and is it the crowd, traffic noise from outside, fans blowing, or TV noise? Do you smell something? More than one something?

Even this exercise itself - trying to pick out the individual elements of a large whole - can feel like a close-to-paralyzing assignment. Therefore, begin with the first thing you notice, and take the time to focus on it before you attempt to discern something else. If you've walked into a conference room for a meeting or some kind of presentation, is the first thing you notice the temperature? Is it cold or hot? Where is the cold or hot air coming from?

Whatever you first take note of, don't dwell on it as something to examine in great detail; note it, and move on to the next thing you notice.

To accomplish this, to take the time to notice and be aware, to accomplish everything that follows, you need to arrive in an environment with enough time to be able to have time.

Give yourself ample time, which means be earlier than on-time. If this will be a struggle for you, if you're habitually 'just barely' making it to appointments on time, or if you always run late, you need to be aware not only of how that affects you, you need to realize how that affects the people and the events that include you. If this will be a new beginning for you -- actually being on time and on schedule – do not strive to make an overnight change. Instead, strive to change, and then consciously, methodically, work at your change.

To take notice, to be aware, you must take time to notice, and you must have time to take.

Be at least on time, and strive to be early.

Move your senses

By move your senses, I mean pay attention to all of them, and as you discover something, focus momentarily on it: smell something, and recognize that you do smell something. Move your eyes and absorb what you see. Hear something? Feel something?

People within a space are integrated with the environment, so you must also observe them, although not to the degree that you make anyone feel uncomfortable. Glance around, and if you make eye-contact, acknowledge that person – don't look away quickly, don't pretend that you didn't glance at him or her – because it's all right. As human beings, we look at each other, sometimes smile, say a quick "hello," or "how's it going," maybe do a simple nod as an acknowledgement. As you have with the other aspects of an environment, make observations about the people around you: any coughers or sneezers; anyone look tired; note-takers; non-note-takers; are there groups? As everyone gathers, are they talking about the same subject? Do you know where everyone was before this meeting or event?

As you consciously work to do this in every environment, you will eventually find that your observations become automatic - the unbreakable habit. As your observations become automatic, everything you sense and observe, the realities of what's inside the space around you, will change how you perceive what you're doing, where you're doing it, and for whom.

If you're a stressed or anxious communicator, perception shifts will eventually replace what your mind sometimes creates during an appearance or presentation: an intimidating thing called an audience, with an expectant, maybe hostile attitude (as your anxiety-occupied mind perceives it, that is). The mind's creation of that scary audience thing is then the catalyst for the physical manifestations of anxiety: excess perspiration, fuzzy eyesight, and sudden inability to hear or think clearly.

The perception shift allows you to accept and embrace the reality around you: an audience is really a group of people just like you, gathered together in a room, ready and willing to hear what you have to say.

Benefits of the Mind Attributes

Development of your awareness enhances your ability to think, speak, and present (Clarity); stay on schedule and deliver your message (Focus); and see the world around you as it really is (Vision).

Don't just develop your unbreakable awareness habit at work, or in work-related situations; do it anytime you move from one environment to another. This is Rehearsal, where specific exercises and repetition lay the foundation for what will eventually become second nature.

The Body Attributes - awareness, balance, breath, flexibility

You have commenced directing your mind to being aware, in a way you have not previously, of your environment. Next, you must become aware of your physical self in every environment.

In Zen, and as a foundation of martial arts, creative and physical arts of dance, athletics, and acting, there is no designation of when to be aware of one's self; there is only awareness.

All of us, are occasionally forced by our bodies to be aware, whether it's by the seizing-up of our lower back, the sharp twinge in our shoulder, or when the inhalation that was supposed to be a deep breath was shortened by a coughing spasm.

Those situations are awareness via urgent biological or physiological message. The body awareness we seek to develop is 'now' awareness, a continuous awareness of physical self.

Take this moment to do a physical assessment. You're probably sitting. Are you:

Slouched?

Bent over?

Resting your chin on one hand?

Sitting with your legs crossed?

Leaning to one side versus the other?

The point here is to assess what you should be aware of, that slouching isn't really good for the back, and neither is being bent over. Supporting our head by resting our chin on one hand may be our normal behavior, but it's not really good for the neck.

A surprise awareness quiz of how we stand, walk, and breathe would reveal other similar variations.

My introduction to martial arts came at a very young age, so through my adolescent, developing years my self-awareness was slightly different than other young men and women my age. One of the habits I never developed was the asymmetric standing posture of more weight supported by one leg than the other, sometimes accompanied by one hand resting on the hip. It's a common sight, all types of people do it: standing on one leg, sometimes dropping into the posture any time they have to stand still, in a cashier's line, or simply standing around and talking with friends.

No one told me not to stand that way, and I can't recall a specific instance where I decided I just wasn't comfortable standing that way.

Imagine my surprise, though, when I entered the Army, and

during the first week of jump school, we received a quick lecture – and demonstration – on what would happen if a Black Hat (fearsome and feared jump instructors) saw anyone, including officers, standing in that fashion: twenty pushups the first time, and any number more for repeat offenders.

Jump school is physically and mentally demanding; balance and body awareness are critical to getting through it, as are accepting the reputation of being a cut above. Aside from what could be construed as conveying a certain attitude by standing in the one-leg, hand-on-hip fashion, it misaligned the body and made it poorly balanced.

"Sheesh," you might be thinking, "who knew?"

Which brings us right back to awareness; now you know.

I can remember only a handful of soldiers who had to perform the first-offense twenty pushups, and there were no repeat offenses. We all quickly became aware of our posture and appearance, and we would also learn just how important body awareness and positioning was to jumping out of a plane without getting hurt. Leaving through the side door of an aircraft flying at 130 knots and looking up four-seconds later to see a fully-inflated parachute canopy required having a certain mind-set, awareness and, before the jump, the correct body position as you stood in the door. The ultimate success of the jump started before the actual jump, and it required an awareness of the environment and the body.

And, if you've just had the thought, "this is about public speaking and presenting, not jumping out of airplanes", I'll point out that there are many people who would rather jump out of an airplane than stand in front of an audience.

Trying to be natural, trying to breathe

Developing the ability to stand naturally, hands out of pockets, for any length of time is an uncomfortable yet required task confronting a beginning actor. Give it a try it for a few minutes during a conversation before you give short shrift to its degree of difficulty.

It feels unnatural. I would also have you try standing in place for one to two minutes, feet spread slightly more than shoulder-width apart, weight evenly distributed, arms at your side.

Physically easy enough to do, but for more of you than not, I'm betting it feels odd. What you're feeling is awareness, an awareness of your posture, muscles, and skeletal structure.

It's an awareness that disappears during a speech or presentation for all but the natural, disciplined, or relaxed public speakers.

But, not every presentation is made standing. Many important decisions, presentations, and sincere speeches are given while seated. Every job interview, whether for an entry-level position or to become CEO, is a seated situation, and for the majority of people, the interview environment will be the most important, pressure-filled presentation they will ever encounter. The vast majority of self-study/self-training information may contain basic guidance for how to dress for and behave during an interview, but there usually isn't much offered in the way of how to stay in touch with your physical self during the process.

The powerful properties of breathing

As if there weren't enough to be aware of within the environment around you, and you in the environment, and how you're standing or sitting, you now have to remember to breathe.

Fair enough if you've just thought, "Hey, I breathe all the time"; 'tis true, but you don't always breathe the right way.

And again, who knew?

When and how you breathe are essential to your comfort level as a presenter. Heck, they're important to your health and well-being throughout life. There are many experts in the cardio fitness field and more than enough accessible information on improving and maintaining cardio fitness, so the focus here is on how important breathing is to being relaxed, responsive, and functional in speaking or presenting situations.

How you breathe affects how you think, act, and react.

Okay, another pop quiz on your physical self-awareness: whether you're sitting, standing, or lying down, is your position helping or hampering your ability to breathe? Yes, if you're reading this, you're breathing; the question goes more to your ability to get the most benefit from breathing. Are you sitting or standing with your shoulders rolled slightly forward, instead of shoulders pulled back, with your chest pulled back and opened? If you're standing, are your shoulders hunched up, tensed? Are your rms folded across your chest? Is your posture slumped?

Compression and contraction, whether from wrapping your arms around your chest or not realizing how tensely you're holding your upper torso, contribute to body-wide tension. Tension is contraction, and contracted muscles contribute to a wide range of negative effects, from general stiffness, to soreness, to more serious situations including fainting. Nervous tension and the physical tension that accompanies it also accelerate a cycle of shallow breathing, and shallow breathing then contributes to a lack of fuel for your muscles. This exacerbates the effects of anxiety and nervousness, and inhibits blood flow to the brain, making it harder to think, to process, to act and react.

To pull together and generalize a phrase used by everyone from musicians to Lamaze partners: breathe, just breathe.

Focus on the breath

Meditation is arguably the ultimate mental method of relaxation, and being aware of your breathing is the first step when learning meditation techniques. I recommend meditation for everyone. Meditation makes you aware of how you breathe, and how you breathe has a direct connection to being an effective communicator.

Anxiety, tension, a rapid heart rate, and other signs of the fight-or-flight response have their roots in the nervous and adrenal systems. How we react to what happens around us starts with the brain, and the perception – right or wrong – of what we see. The body's reactions to stressful situations are in large part hardwired within the brain's primal areas. In a stressful situation, our respiratory rate increases. While an elevated respiratory rate might seem to assist in getting more air in and out of our lungs, rapid respiration breaths are commonly shallow, and unless we actually do take flight, and engage our lungs through the physical motion of fleeing, those rapid, shallow breaths can leave a person lightheaded. They also dry the mouth and the back of the throat, making it difficult to speak.

But, reactions to stressful situations can be altered significantly through training.

Rehearsal is training

Boxers and martial artists train extensively – and training is analogous to rehearsing - to develop a specific response to stimuli, like slipping a punch coming at the face, responding defensively and continually programming themselves until the response is reflexive. To get to that point, however, they need to rehearse the situation over and over, training first their brain and then further developing their physical response, until it all becomes truly automatic.

Firefighters, doctors, and athletes, all rehearse situations, again and again, to overcome mental and physical challenges. As a paratrooper, intense jump school training includes heavy repetition, to reinforce behavior and response. From the earliest days of training, many of the exercises for 'getting out the door' of a plane, initially on a ground level platform, then out of a thirty-foot tower, then out of the plane itself, are performed with a jump master standing beside the student jumper at the door. The jump master controls the exit of each trooper. Here again, what will eventually happen 'for real' starts with the end in mind during the earliest days of training.

As the paratrooper steps into the door, he or she waits for the shouted command "Go!" from the jump master before leaping out. In jump school, through all the exercises, the training jump master is there to shout "go", and deliver a hard slap on the ass of the trainee, a physical cue that reinforces the oral command.

The instructors at Ft. Benning's jump school are intense and very fit, and I recall that many a hard slap was a hard slap. The majority of us, after our first jump from the airplane during the final week of jump school, had no recollection of that slap as we jumped, even though we saw the jump master do it to everyone in front of us.

We had been conditioned to the point that even in our first real jump environment, when the door opened, accompanied by a roar of the sucking wind and deafening engine noise, creating what could rightfully be called a psychologically overwhelming environment, we stopped at the door, got our "Go!" and we went.

Most of us were afraid to varying degrees, but while we felt fear, we did as we had been trained, correctly, in spite of our fight or flight situation (pun intended).

With self-awareness, awareness of your environment, and by successfully using techniques you've practiced, you can present or speak even if you have not completely diffused your nervousness or anxiety.

Breathing your internal rhythm

Breathing properly is a key component of awareness, and it's essential for physical and mental mobility.

I started this book by describing us as a sense-oriented species. What we also are, though, is a metronome. Inside every one of us is a continual, variable, beating metronome. A good, strong heart can maintain a consistent heart rate for extended periods of time. It varies with internal and external situations, but we all have a natural rhythm. Some are more aware than others, in a literal and figurative way, of that internal rhythm; regardless, we all have it.

Not many of us realize that we can, within limits, exert some control over our internal rhythm. We can assist our heart in slowing down when we're amped up. We can accomplish this with our breathing, by understanding a technique called *focus on the breath*.

Focus on the breath is more than just knowing that you're breathing; by concentrating on the fact that you are breathing, and concentrating on how it feels to inhale and exhale, a calmness settles the mind, as heart and respiratory rates slow to a steady pace, and muscle tension ebbs. It's analogous to an exhalation after a tense situation, as when a student reads through a long list of test results, finally finds that she passed, and releases a long, audible sigh. That release is a physical and mental release of tension. Focusing on the breath and consciously breathing at a steady, relaxed rate is also a release of tension, but in a controlled, continuous, sustained manner.

When one sits in meditation, it's important for the back to be straight, with the shoulders naturally pulled back so the body is aligned and breathing is easy. The posture allows the body maximum use of oxygen, which includes a steady flow of oxygenated blood to the brain, which improves cognitive function.

"It helps ya think." That's a pretty simple explanation for the complicated processes that go on inside us.

The easiest way to develop an awareness of your breathing is to include it on the list of awareness attributes we've pointed out thus far. Take that moment where you are absorbing the sights and sounds of the physical environment, your place in it, and the people around you. Now check-in and make sure you're not holding your breath.

You'll be surprised initially by how many times you discover that you are holding your breath, or not breathing in and out fully. You'll be more surprised to discover that the actual thought itself, "am I holding my breath?" may actually make you hold your breath!

It's a sign that somewhere along the way you developed a trait that many people share: at certain points when performing a task – be it physical or mental - you hold your breath. Whether leaping to catch a pass, learning how to dance, loosening a rusty lug nut, or finding just the right words to place on a PowerPoint slide, fluid motion and fluid thought can't occur without proper blood flow and oxygen.

So here's another multi-component addition to your unbreakable habit list during this rehearsal phase: check your breath, check your body. You now know to be aware of yourself, the room, and the people; now be aware of your breath and your body.

When you check on your breath, start your check-in process with a slightly longer, slightly deeper inhale than what you perceive to be your 'normal' breath (in meditation this is sometimes called a cleansing breath), pause for a moment, and then exhale in a controlled, easy manner. As you do this, you may be surprised to find that you can already feel what your posture is like, so go ahead and flow with that: hold your head up, stand a bit straighter, let your shoulders relax, let them settle, and then gently pull them back slightly and open your chest.

Take a few more breaths like that. Make a conscience effort

to breathe a touch deeper, in and out, and to sense that you are a bit more relaxed.

When you're a bit more relaxed, you'll find that your awareness is once again enhanced, that you feel a bit more in control.

Now that you have awareness and control, it's time to check your flexibility.

Uh-huh, really.

And our breathing leads us to flexibility...

...because without proper breathing, there can't be flexibility. Mental and physical flexibility are what give you the ability to answer a question correctly, without hesitation (because you know your content, as we'll go over later in the Performance section). They allow you to make a graceful, micro-second, injury-preventing adjustment as you walk to the podium and your foot hits a slick spot on the stage. Flexibility gives you the freedom to move naturally as you speak, so you can allow your emotions to drive your mannerisms, instead of looking like the under-trained or over-trained spokesperson whose movements look like they were choreographed by a dancing robot (more about that later, too).

The optimal way to achieve physical flexibility, and the benefits or drawbacks of stretching routines, are still occasionally debated among fitness professionals and researchers, but there is no argument as to the overall benefits of having muscles that are loose, relaxed, and able to respond or act in a fluid manner. Amazingly, if the body is tense, a person can injure themselves doing the most mundane things.

Many years ago, as I was hanging pictures in an office hallway, I let the hammer drop the few feet to the floor. It landed with a thunk just as one of the office managers walked around a corner. It startled her, and as she reflexively hopped away from the sound, she said, "Oww, I hurt my neck."

She carried so much tension in her body that her own slight but sudden movement caused her pain (it wasn't serious; it also didn't change her tense personality).

Breathing and flexibility can't truly be separated. Yoga, the ultimate approach to stretching, may be the most accessible example of how the merging of breath and stretching provides ultimate flexibility of mind and body, but even basic approaches to fitness and relaxation include the importance of both warming up and breathing when performing exercises.

Don't hold your breath.

The flexible mind

Maintaining a flexible mind is means having the mental flexibility to move, react, act or change your presentation as you're giving it.

A great example of this occurred on live television in what could be the most high-profile, pressure-cooker environment possible, a State of the Union Address.

President Clinton had entered the House and made his way to the podium. As he acknowledged the applause and prepared to speak, he looked at the teleprompter screen and realized that the opening lines displayed were from a different speech than the one he was about to give. As the ovation ebbed, he turned quickly to Vice President Gore, seated behind him, and said, "It's the wrong speech."

None of this would be known until afterwards, but everyone could see that something was happening. It didn't appear as anything very worrisome, even though Gore did look slightly concerned as he leaned forward to better hear the President.

Clinton had started to turn back to the podium as Gore leaned forward, and in response to Gore's "What?" Clinton turned back quickly and said, "The teleprompter has the wrong speech." President Clinton then faced the House, spread out the printed pages of the speech he'd carried as a backup, and began speaking as Gore left his seat to fix the situation.

Gore came back less than a minute later, and the correct speech quickly rolled across the teleprompter.

Here's a review of what happened, and why mental flexibility matters: a tiny mistake (wrong file) in a place with such control and redundancy it should never have happened (the highest level of government) that could have caused grand embarrassment (the leader of the free world, on live television), was all negated by a simple but necessary tool (a printed copy of the speech), and the presenter's preparation and ability to react (flexibility).

Get into that habit

You have taken your first steps; you are more aware. You must continue to rehearse what you've learned as we move to the next section, Run Thru.

As with anything you wish to master, you will have to work at developing your unbreakable habit of awareness. As you develop it, you will discover that you work less and less to be aware, and your concerted efforts to be aware will *become* awareness.

Section Two - Run Thru

Get Ready for the Real Thing

Because you're going to have to do it anyway

You hear the final words of your introduction.

Or

The room is full, it's nine-o'clock in the morning, you're at the front of the room and it's time to start the presentation.

Or

Your team has taken their seats at the conference table, everyone has coffee, chit-chat has died down, and in a few moments you'll provide marketing information to the handful of executives who have the go-ahead to select or reject you as their vendor of choice.

There could be factors over which you have no control in any of those scenarios, and which could prevent you from achieving your goal, from bias or under-the-table relationships to power outages or a bad microphone cable.

All of which may doom your future...at least temporarily.

It doesn't matter.

Oh, I know it does matter, in the sense that no one wants to look goofy, sound stupid, or fail to 'make the grade'.

It doesn't matter because you must present anyway. Objectively, I accept that you can call in sick, refuse to do the presentation, stop in the middle of everything and go home; all of those and other actions of free will allow you to not give the presentation. But, let's deal in the reality of our lives, to wit: you can obsess, fuss, whine, worry, sweat, swear, procrastinate, and believe for all you're worth that the presentation is going to be a disaster, and none of that matters, because you will have to do the presentation anyway.

All the worrying and obsessing will only ensure that you either give a lousy presentation, or you'll do a fine presentation but be a psychological or physical wreck from all the obsessing you did that wasn't going to matter because...you had to give the presentation.

I performed in many school plays, back when dinosaurs walked the planet and I was in high school. During one dress rehearsal, I became distracted and realized that I had missed a cue for my character's entrance. I ran through the set's doorway and into a scene suspended in time, with several actors standing in place, silently, awaiting my entrance to move the scene forward. From the darkness at the back of the auditorium came the disembodied voice of our drama instructor, Mr. C., who said loudly and with just the perfect degree of sarcasm, "Thank you."

It was a lesson never lost on me, on so many levels, including that no one else can play your part, so you better show up.

Another lesson from that incident is to keep your head in the game, and only in the game. Focus on what needs to be done, not on what could happen if you don't get it done well, or what might happen if you forget your lines, or if you get confused.

You have to do the presentation anyway, so put your head to work on that. What may or may not happen is of no consequence to you having to do the presentation, so develop it, prep for it, put it together and do it. Whatever may or may not happen from that – even if you and your team know this is the opportunity of a lifetime, which increases the pressure to get everything 'more' than right – conjecturing about what may or may not result from the presentation will not make the presentation better, but it could certainly make it worse.

Accept this shift in your thinking: be true to the task at hand, concentrate on it and not on what doesn't exist (the things that *might* happen, the "yeah, but what if..." thoughts, etc.), and the result will be success.

It can be very difficult to accept at first. Understand that I am not advocating a development process that ignores conflicts, contingencies, or potential problems. Just the opposite; every potential problem must be planned for, but the distraction of conjecture – the "what if I screw this up?" – serves only to take energy and focus away from the development process.

"What if the power goes out?" is a realistic possibility, though unlikely. If it's a major power outage there will be nothing you can do about it.

"What if the projector doesn't work?" is a realistic possibility, with higher probability. A back-up projector or an overhead projector and a set of transparencies are smart, well-planned and proactive solutions.

"What if I sound/look/feel stupid, or they don't like me?" and other alike thoughts have very little to do with the reality of creating effective communications. You may have some legitimate physical, mental, or health-related issues that challenge your ability to speak or be heard by an audience, and these would be genuine situations to take into consideration. Presentation anxiety, stage fright, or shyness may, to the sufferer, seem no less of a challenge, but are overcome by training and work. They are not addressed nor overcome by worrying about them.

Be true, do the work – on the presentation and on yourself – and everything will be fine.

The world is your trainer, every day

In Section One - Rehearsal, you became more aware of yourself and your surroundings, and you learned how your enhanced awareness provides a more realistic perspective on environments and the people in them (i.e., remember that an audience is actually a group of people who are interested in what you have to say).

We're now going to use the people and surroundings in your daily life to prepare you for your next communications project or situation. We'll build on your self-awareness, incorporate all the attributes of Mind and Body, and bring in exercises you can do throughout your day to develop, enhance and strengthen your communication skills.

Awareness every day

"It can be a tough audience. They're judging you the moment they see you. They'll even look to see what kind of watch you're wearing." (A labor consultant, talking about presenting to a mostly blue-collar workforce)

36

Let's once again start at a beginning, the beginning that occurs before you even wake-up, the beginning where you are already taking care of your health, where you have incorporated into your daily life some form of regular exercise – walking, yoga, golf, masters swimming program - because you know it's good for your body and your brain. You're also eating with a more healthy-foods approach, and you're not doing things to yourself, mentally or physically, in any fashion or to any extent that they are allowed to interfere with the overall quality of your life.

That's the beginning you've already begun.

Now let's wake up and hit the day as a communicator.

Wow, you look...

How you think you look is important, yes, but because you're on a path to better self-awareness as a communicator, how you look and how you want others to perceive you are of equal importance.

The people you interact with throughout your day will, right or wrong, form an opinion of you based on your: looks, clothes, personality, skin color, accent, tone of voice, body shape, your car, your neighborhood, cigarette smoking, gum chewing, mannerisms, heritage, what you drink, if you drink...

All of those are slices of the whole, and the whole is this - you will be judged.

For you as a communicator, and as a human being, there are things you can change about yourself and your lifestyle; things you can change with varying degrees of difficulty; and things you can't change at all. If changing some things about yourself will take you along a path of being a better person, do it.

But do not change what you shouldn't; do not accept or discard anything that diminishes your humanity; and do not condone nor promote, by word, deed or thought, the diminishment of another's humanity.

This is the mantel you must shoulder, the standard to which you continually aspire. Here it is again: Do not change what you shouldn't; do not accept or discard anything that diminishes your humanity; and do not condone nor promote, by word, deed or thought, the diminishment of another's humanity.

37

As you dress and prepare for the day, find the balance in your presentation of yourself. You need to be physically and mentally comfortable; be aware of what's appropriate for the environments you'll be in; and present yourself in a manner that shows your respect for your audience, be it a team, manager, CEO, store clerk, teacher, or friend.

For several decades, the four members of the internationally-respected Modern Jazz Quartet (known as MJQ), no matter the venue or the size of the audience, dressed in impeccable suits or tuxedos for every performance. A member explained in an interview that people had paid money to see MJQ perform, and, in return, the group owed the audience respect and appreciation. It was the return on the audience's investment of money and time. MJQ was able to do what they loved, and the least they could do was show how appreciative they were of the people who supported them.

Be yourself, but put the audience at your forefront. Find the balance in being yourself while communicating, at every opportunity, that you appreciate and respect your audience.

(for tips and guidance about how to judge what you should wear, and of certain things to be aware of – i.e., polish your shoes (you too, ladies) – go to thewaytocommunicate.com)

You look good; how do you smell?

I once had to answer an unusually difficult question from a client, difficult because it dealt with a personal, lifestyle situation. My client's firm was engaged in HR work for a hospital, and part of the work included giving several presentations to health care professionals. My client was evaluating which of his senior consultants to bring in on the project, and asked if I believed a particular consultant's cigarette smoking would interfere with his ability to effectively communicate.

My answer was "Yes." My answer was based on several factors, including the workplace environment, the audience, the audience's perceptions, and on how the effectiveness of the presenter could be compromised by the smell of cigarettes. It was not based on my personal feelings about people who smoke.

This is a sensitive matter, with individual rights and personal habits issues, but, objectively, my concerns were the same as they would be if it was about someone who smoked cigars or a pipe, chewed tobacco, dipped snuff, chewed gum, wore perfume, cologne, or aftershave. To a non-smoker, the smell of cigarette, cigar, or pipe tobacco is easily noticed, just as people who don't wear cologne, aftershave or perfume may be much more sensitive to their presence. Regular smokers carry the scent of smoke on their clothes. Someone who doesn't use a fragrance can easily detect someone who does.

Gum chewing, while not overtly approaching the more sensitive levels of individual rights, can be maddeningly distracting. No one who interacts with the public on a professional basis, from cashier to department director, should do so with a chunk of gum dancing around their (occasionally open while they're chewing) mouth.

Communication is compromised by distraction, whether it is the concrete distraction of noise, smell, something visual, or an abstract, psychological distraction. A communicator can do little to prevent an observer from judging on the basis of personal bias, but the effective communicator should be willing to take all the elements of an environment into consideration in choosing to do or not do certain things. This includes smoking, chewing tobacco, using snuff, nose picking, spitting, or anything of questionable appropriateness.

In the case of my client, speaking to health care workers while carrying the scent of cigarettes into an otherwise pristine environment would create a distraction and diminish the presenter's effectiveness.

The purpose of abstaining from an action in a public speaking or presentation environment is not to prevent you from being yourself, it's to avoid creating a distraction or challenge to be overcome even before saying "Hi, good to see you today."

Initial Eye Contact - Let everyone know you're a communicator
When you look people in the eye you convey a very important message directly to them: "I recognize your existence."

You validate their life for that moment.

Don't interpret looking someone in the eye as staring them

down, and don't compromise your safety when eye contact might be considered as an inadvertent challenge or delivery of a silent, symbolic message. The point of initial eye contact is to offer recognition of someone, and invite recognition in return.

I studiously attempt to avoid promoting one business over another, but I'm making an exception here. Many years ago I worked part-time at Borders' bookstore in San Rafael, California.

Booksellers, as we were called, worked the cashier line, restocked books, and, my favorite task, worked at the customer service kiosk, where customers inquired about books and placed special orders. When I looked at customers and said, "Hi, how are you," or "What can I do for you today?" as they approached the counter, they responded in kind. Is this an earth-shaking revelation? No, but it's a valuable lesson in establishing a connection. Seems simplistic, I know, but it's the key to everything in this book. Heck, it's the way I began this book.

The simple act of watching a person approach the counter, making eye contact and then opening my communication door by extending an invitation – "Hi, how are you? Want to talk about something?" – began our dialog, and there can't be a dialog without a connection.

Did it change the world? Did people who had a complaint, were having a bad day, didn't give a hoot about anything outside of their own existence, did it make things all better? Certainly not, but it was almost always a positive experience, and created a positive, active communications environment.

I began the interaction and therefore, at least initially, controlled it, not in a draconian or Foghorn Leghorn sense, but because I initiated it I set the tone, the feel, and the direction of the dialog.

I invited interaction. My opening was a figurative, outstretched helping hand to open a beneficial conversation.

By making initial eye contact I validated and recognized the person's existence. My greeting conveyed that at some level I cared. I wanted to assist, and I made that known in word, tone, posture, gesture and attitude.

BUT...

Yes, there's a but: not everyone wants to make eye contact,

not everyone wants to be recognized, and not everyone cares about you or your willingness to communicate.

So be it. You will have to learn the cues and signals from people who decline your communication invitation. I believe, however, that most people will respond positively to your glance, smile, nod or spoken "Hi".

Whether it's in your company's hallways, on a sidewalk, in a store, or entering a reception populated by people you don't know, you are well-served by smiling and saying hello.

It will make you a better communicator, especially if you...

Listen - You started it, now you've got to remain in it

You opened the communications door, or maybe someone asked you to open it – "Got a minute, Mike?" – so along with maintaining great eye contact, you have to listen.

You have to listen with everything you've got.

You know what I mean? Ever been locked into a conversation and all you could think about was how to escape? It happens. Not that it's all right, but it does happen.

In several different interviews, musician Billy Joel has explained his reluctance to perform some of his biggest but older hits during concerts. He described how one night while performing he caught himself in a most mundane thought as he was singing: "*I wonder what I should eat after the show?*" It took him by surprise, even though working musicians who perform certain songs throughout many years of touring struggle to overcome their own form of story fatigue (described in section three, Performance).

Imagine being so bored or distracted that you're not even listening to yourself!

He stopped performing certain songs until he could revisit them with a fresher appreciation for the song and the audience.

When you commit to listen, you can't impose your will or personality on anyone, so you can't make someone get to their point quicker – you can assist them in getting to their point, by asking appropriate questions, or supplying information, but in doing that, the most important thing NOT to do is to finish their sentences for them.

Most of the time you'll be wrong, it makes the dialog awkward, and it can be just downright rude. If you interject – you have a quick thought about something - give them a signal before you speak; raise your hand as if you were stopping traffic, but don't be obnoxious about it, and when they pause, say "I don't want to interrupt, but didn't we/aren't we/ (or whatever it is)..." and then help the person remember where to pick up the thread of their sentence again.

As a communicator, you should willingly open your communicating door, and commit to the conversation at hand. If it is a conversation from which you need to disengage, for whatever reason, you need to do that in a legitimate manner.

It's okay; we work and live in a jam-packed-overly-scheduled world. The way to disengage legitimately is to state the legitimate reason: "Jimmy, I've got a meeting upstairs in three minutes, so I'll make sure we connect later to talk about this."

There are also those ambush situations, sometimes inadvertent on the ambusher, sometimes not. The tripwire for this is any variation of "Got a minute?" Whether you have a minute or not, give them the truth, and a bonus: "For you, I've got two minutes." Plan for three to four minutes, then, "I'm going to work on this, find an answer, and, is it all right if I email you?"

or

"I have to/I'm in a (whatever it is), and I'll call you back at (a time you know you will)."

A legitimate reason to cut short or postpone a conversation won't be hurtful, and facilitates better communication when you meet-up again with that same person (unless you've been using the same reason to avoid any conversation opportunity with that person).

If there isn't a meeting, emergency, conflict, or anything else hanging over the conversation you've initially committed to, then you can be direct, but not insensitive: "Barb, I understand, but right now I've got some things I've got to take care of; let's schedule some time to talk about this."

The reality of life is that we must occasionally interact with people even as we desperately want to be or need to be somewhere else. That's an aspect of being human. Another aspect of being human is empathy; the person you might desperately wish to not interact with may feel that what they want to share with you is of extreme importance, and you should give them their moment. Commit to a moment of their life and, more often than not, your own life will be better for it.

Balance every day - You move, act, and react, because you're balanced, aware, and ready.

Let's pick-up from the previous advice on listening.

In that listening situation from which you wanted to flee, but made the commitment to stay and listen – at least for a moment – you maintained eye contact, you listened, you responded... but how were you standing, and what were you doing?

Were you leaning away from the person, or standing straight?

Were your arms at your sides, hands out of your pockets, or in your pocket fiddling with change or keys?

As you interact with people – in the parking lot, coming through the office doors, in a meeting room, at the grocery store – what kind of signals does your posture send? What do people assume about you because of the way you walk or move?

Balance, mental and physical, is a key that fits many locks. Your body language communicates messages constantly. You can't prevent someone from misinterpreting what many other people would interpret correctly, but you can work diligently to control people's perceptions of you based on your posture and physical attitude.

A person's body language is, at times, a true external indicator of how he or she feels emotionally. One of the first body language signals I learned to interpret, and I believe the first most people learn, is that arms folded across the chest is an outward sign of someone's emotional defensiveness, as in not agreeing with, or not being receptive to, what they're hearing or seeing. As often as this may accurately represent someone's feelings, it may also be that the person is cold; or crossing their arms is a comfortable habit; or it could be a reaction to something they're thinking about that has nothing to do with anything presently going on around them!

You may have some posture habits that people interpret as attitude and, as described above, you may not even be aware that you lean, stand, or fidget in a particular way. The phrase "that's a tell" refers to the close-to-imperceptible, physical mannerisms that reveal the strength or weakness of a poker player's cards. The phrase has entered the cultural lexicon through the immense popularity of poker-based reality TV shows.

While the "tell" may, on occasion, provide an observer with signals about an opponent's hand of cards, it is less than a science and highly subjective.

For the communicator, whether you have a tell or not is not as important as whether or not you are projecting an impression of a tell. We may not always be able to disguise or control our slightly trembling hands when we're nervous, or prevent the reflection of light caused by the fine sheen of perspiration on our forehead, but what we can do is strive to find our mental and physical balance. Stepping into and being aware of our balanced body position – feet slightly more than shoulder-width apart, relaxed but straight posture (don't lock your knees if you're going to have to stand for a length of time), shoulders relaxed – are reminders to be balanced internally and externally.

Stand in a relaxed but open, balanced posture and face people when you interact with them. If it's uncomfortably awkward for you to stand with your arms at your side, and it's a casual situation, you can put your hands in your pockets. Make an effort not to fold your arms across your chest.

Pay attention to how people around you walk, sit, converse and listen. Think about the perceptions you have and assumptions you make about people based on their posture. If you're in an environment that allows for repeated observations, like a multi-day conference where you'll see many of the same people several times, remember what you believed about someone based on your observations, and look for opportunities to judge yourself on the accuracy, or inaccuracy, of your assumptions.

Clarity - Make the world you're in as clear as you can

Clarity is a mental state of unhindered focus and awareness

that facilitates the ability to understand, evaluate, decide and act without hesitation.

As a communicator, clarity allows you to constantly monitor and process everything around you, and inside you. The way to clarity begins with effort, develops via sustained practice and study, and evolves to become a moment-to-moment mastery of simultaneous observation, process, and response.

Hoo-boy.

It's not really magic, but it does feel special when you actually experience it. The simplest description of clarity is to know instantly.

When you have clarity, you project clarity; your message and your delivery are concise, easy to understand, and your message becomes easy to grasp.

When you are clear, a greater percentage of your audience understands your message.

Being aware encompasses being informed, and both contribute to clarity.

The ability to deliver a concise message, to have an answer for every question, and to know where answers are when you get the never-before-asked-or-considered question, these are requirements for the effective communicator. Knowledge is the platform from which you establish yourself as a credible authority on your message, and that authority puts people at ease. An audience at ease is an audience that listens.

Begin each day with the intention of achieving clarity in your purpose'for the next twenty-four hours. In the beginning, you may actually find yourself concentrating so intently on certain things that you miss what's going on around you, or your colleagues and friends let you know you seem distracted.

Improving your awareness of the environment around you, and of yourself in it, enhances your effort to achieve clarity, as do studying and learning. As you move through the day, monitor everything around you, recognize who and what you see, and train your brain to locate and make connections related to who and what you see, and to what you experience.

Unexpectedly run into a co-worker in the lobby? If you have a meeting that involves that co-worker, make a mind-statement about that. Think, "I'm seeing Mary at the project review this morning; I've got to make sure I have her latest report in the folder."

Consciously making the mind-statement is programming for your brain. More than a reminder, it's a form of thought that builds an internal networking schema, and eventually programs your brain to recognize something or someone, then seek, link to and retrieve all the pertinent information related to what you observe.

You can achieve your own level of clarity in whatever you choose.

Connecting, awareness, and knowledge lead to clarity

Knowing about the world, the country, the neighborhood, the economy, popular culture, current events, history, and keeping track of your friends' remodeling project, their kids' soccer games, your co-workers' vacations, all of this should be part of your new sense of awareness. But it's nearly impossible to keep track of everything, even when you scale it down to just knowing what's happening in the lives of the people around you. You may have no idea who that world leader was on the news last night, but with every effort you make to be aware of what's happening, the more attuned you become to what people believe is important, and to understanding why they feel the way they do. When you know what makes people feel or behave in a certain way, you become more empathetic, one of the most important traits of an effective communicator.

I have always been an avid reader, and I have always wanted to know what was going on, everywhere. I am still confused, and a bit saddened as I grow older, by otherwise intelligent, caring people who choose not to follow news in any of its forms, whether via the Web, newspapers, or TV news programs. Many willingly agree that their rationale for self-enforced naiveté is personal, and logically weak, but they hold strongly to the belief that being news-aware, with what they perceive to be a leaning by the media towards scandal, tragedy and hyperbole, only makes them feel sad, inadequate, or simply doesn't contribute to their lives in a positive way.

I am not dismissive, nor should you be, of their attitude, because the news-naiveté lifestyle is in itself very revealing about the person who chooses not to be informed in that manner.

As a communicator, however, you must be informed. To communicate, you must understand; to understand, you must be able to see all the facets of what must be understood.

The ability to see and understand all facets of an environment or situation is clarity.

Having an awareness of things, having an attitude of wanting to know more, or wanting to understand the push and the pull of an event or situation, can give you that sense of clarity, and it is this same kind of knowing that brings clarity to you as a communicator.

Content - Know what you should, give your audience what they want...but not always what they expect

The keys to assembling and delivering great content are gathering information directly related to the content, while maintaining awareness about the intended audience's point-of-view on the subject.

As a communicator, the better you know, the better you flow. When you have the right content your audience is a sponge. An audience becomes a sponge for your content not just because it's a message in which they have an interest, but because the content directly relates to the audience's point of view on the message.

For several years I taught an all-encompassing video production class at a commercial school in the Bay Area. With every new group of students came a handful of recurring commonalities. When it came time to assign the first short documentary on a subject of each student's choosing, at least a handful from every class initially wanted to do a documentary on "the homeless".

I used this recurring situation as an opportunity to explain how to form, clarify, and focus a valid documentary idea. I described the different points-of-view of the Bay Area's homeless situation: numbers (estimated 5,000 homeless people; 2,500 to

5,000 teenage homeless; homeless families); money (programs for the homeless; costs to the city related to homelessness; merchant concerns over potential revenue losses connected to homelessness-related issues); education (education for homeless children; adult literacy, job skills training), crime committed by/to homeless)...

There were many more issues than I list here. Students began to understand not only how any of those perspectives might have some appeal to a general audience, but how by focusing on a specific element of the complex "plight of the homeless" subject, the story would appeal to people with an interest in that particular point-of-view.

The importance of this lecture was that for many students it was their first understanding as visual storytellers that they should consider their message's audience. By studying all the facets of a subject, they could clarify their idea and connect to their particular audience. In the realm of professional storytelling, content is both for and about the audience.

As you move through your day, think about the audience perspective of any message you're delivering, whether the audience comprises members of your project team, the public at large, your customer base, or you're simply trying to find out from a cashier why your local big-store no longer carries a certain kind of whachamajigger. The young cashier in that big-store's department probably doesn't know why, so pointed questions or admonitions won't get you anywhere, while a conversation with the department manager might (it will still be a stretch in many cases...).

On The Way to Communicate website you can read a great example about matching content to an audience in a most creative fashion. It's from Lou Naidorf, a lifetime-achievement awarded architect. During his forty-year career with one of history's greatest, modern architectural firms, Welton-Beckett, in Los Angeles, he designed several buildings which are now iconic, and in several cases define the skylines of their cities: the Dallas Hyatt, a futuristic building with reflective skin and a

landmark, sphere-topped tower; the Valley National Bank building in downtown Phoenix, for decades the tallest building west
of the Mississippi; and, most iconic of all, the Capitol Records
building in Hollywood, its cylindrical shape known all over the
world, and, remarkably, Lou's first commercial design project as a
commercial architect at the age of twenty-three (nope, it was not
designed to look like a stack of records).

He is a wonderful communicator. Go to thewaytocommuni-
cate.com to read Lou's recollection of the day he pulled together
the most remarkable content-driven lecture of which I've ever
personally heard.

Knowing the subject is only part of the secret to great content; knowing the audience is the key to creating solid, interesting, and relevant content. It requires selecting a perspective on a
subject that will connect with your particular audience.

Empathy - We're all in this together
"Well, what do you think?"

It's a question that's asked about everything from bad sports
calls to important business deals. It's also asked about people,
about an interviewee, about the salesperson and the product after
a demonstration, or any number of different human interaction
situations.

But when it's being asked about a person, our answer is often
based on how we feel about the person. Our answer to "What do
you think about her?" is almost certainly an answer to the un-
asked but assumed question, how do we feel about her.

Having an emotional response, a feeling for someone, or for
someone's particular situation, is based on our empathy, the quality of feeling a kinship with another person based on a shared or
similar emotional experience. Sympathy is feeling sorry for someone; empathy is feeling with someone, when our own reaction is
based on having been in an analogous situation and recalling our
own emotional response.

Author Daniel Goleman wrote Emotional Intelligence
twenty years ago, a groundbreaking book about emotional
development and its role in our professional and personal lives.
It has been in print continuously since its initial release and has

sold over five-million copies worldwide. In the book, Goleman says, "...I serve as a guide through [the] scientific insights into emotions, a voyage aimed at bringing greater understanding to some of the most perplexing moments in our own lives and in the world around us." Significant portions of the book focus on empathy, how and when it develops, why some people have more empathy than others, and how it affects and influences our lives. Everyone should read this important book.

Goleman also references the work of prominent psychologists researching emotions and emotional development. He shares this description of empathy from Dr. Peter Salovey and Dr. John Mayer: Empathy, [an] ability that builds on emotional self-awareness, is the fundamental "people skill...People who are empathetic are more attuned to the subtle social signals that indicate what others need or want. This makes them better at callings such as the caring professions, teaching, sales, and management."

I now add communicator to that list.

You can't truly be an effective communicator without empathy.

Be aware of your thoughts and observations towards people around you. Don't try to read minds, but do be aware of your reactions to how someone talks to you, looks at you, or ignores you. If you see someone who seems to be scowling, is your initial thought, "Wow, someone's grumpy," or is it "Wow, wonder what's happening in his life that makes him feel that way."

For your development as a communicator (and in striving to have a more humanitarian outlook in general), train your response to people so that you first recognize the common connection that we all have to each other. As we move through adulthood, we all share a lifetime of living experiences, from getting a promotion, to kissing the bruise on our child's finger to make it all better, to losing a member of our family. That scowling person may be someone who's often more grumpy than pleasant, but there are a legion of reasons why that might be, from having a sore toe to getting a diagnosis of cancer.

50

Don't shut the communication door based on any assumption.

I was once with the owner of a billion-dollar company as he prepared to go to his company's holiday party. The party was at a facility only a few minutes away, and as the owner left his office I noted that he was going to be there almost twenty minutes early. He said, "I know, but I want to make sure I'm there when my people show up."

He didn't say his employees, he said "his people". He wanted to be there when they walked in the room to show he cared about them. They may have been his company's employees, but he used this and other opportunities to communicate his feelings for them as the people in his company. And, as I observed during subsequent opportunities, his people truly liked and respected him.

Conversations, shared recollections, sharing confidences, laughing about common experiences, these are all about feelings, emotions, and connections we universally share. Empathy contributes to your ability to communicate. People can feel an intangible but real connection when they recognize that quality in someone, and when they feel it, they, in turn, want to communicate.

Flexibility & Focus - Life as a balance beam

A gymnastic balance beam is just wide enough to accommodate the width of an average-size foot. Placed on a floor, even someone with size 12-D feet can manage to walk along its length.

Elevate that beam four-feet above the floor, though, and things change. The beam itself doesn't change at all; it remains sixteen-feet long, and just over four-inches wide. The differences between the person who walks successfully across the raised beam, the person who doesn't, and the gymnast who flips, leaps, and spins from one end of the beam to the other, are balance, state-of-mind, and maintaining both via flexibility and focus.

For us mere mortals, our challenge is to concentrate on moving across the beam and not be distracted by thoughts of what may happen if we fall. Concentrating on moving across the beam is our focus.

Because we are human, not machine, we will make mental and physical miscalculations as we move which interfere with our effort to stay on the beam. We will fail to place our foot or feet over the center of the beam, or we may dip our shoulders and throw off our center of gravity. We will make quick adjustments to our physical position to remain stable on the beam. Balance keeps us stable and on a steady course, but our ability to adjust quickly and regain or maintain our balance is our flexibility.

The difference between those of us who can move along the beam's length when it's on the floor, when it's four-feet above the floor, and moving through a front somersault followed by a leaping scissors kick, are the degrees of flexibility and focus.

As communicators, we focus on delivering a message. Because we're human, we must work to keep our balance as we communicate. If something occurs that breaks our concentration, within us or around us, we must refocus quickly. Our ability to react, compensate, and recover from distractions or missteps, requires an ability to maintain or regain focus. The quick shift to recovery requires mental and physical flexibility.

During a live, solo performance I did about my work in a hurricane Katrina shelter, I looked at the audience and saw someone who seemed on the edge of a nap. Later during the same performance I could hear someone sitting close to the stage, making audible "mmm-hmmm" noises in agreement with what I was saying. During a performance several weeks later, a cell phone rang in the audience as I was reaching a climactic point in the final minutes of the show.

I have been around long enough to accept that these things happen, to take note of them as they happen, and continue with whatever I'm doing. (There are things that happen, like equipment falling over, or technical glitches, that must be recognized and addressed by the communicator to the audience; I will expand on these situations in the Performance section.)

Such is the ebb and flow of life performance, whether it's a laptop freezing up during a demo, someone in the audience breaking into a raging coughing fit, or a table falling off the edge of a riser in the company's trade show booth. An ability to focus, and having the mental and physical flexibility to shift your thoughts, to think on your feet, are a foundation for successfully continuing to communicate during and after these distractions.

As with so much else in life, with effort and practice you can achieve high degrees of focus and flexibility. The ability to have thoughts unrelated to what you're doing, to notice something out of the norm while you continue your presentation or conversation, comes with practice and experience.

Vision - Getting to what you see

"This is what I always dreamed of, Michael."

Pat Morrow was walking along the back side of the multi-level stage. It, and the entire show, were state of the art for their time and function. The stage was well over ten feet high at the drum riser, with eighty-foot runways along the stage's back edge, curving out and around the right and left wings.

Pat, Journey's road manager, smiled and shared his thoughts with me, but the dream he referred to wasn't the high-profile, glitzy, endless parties, Hollywood News Tonight kind of rockstardom dream; his dream was about having been part of a unique vision becoming reality.

At that moment, every phase of the show was set, on schedule, and working the way it should. The audience would pack the stadium and take part in a great social gathering, with music, lights, sound and emotion.

For the moment, an hour before the start of the show, no one was running around frantically, there were no problems, everything was working and ready to go. Pat was allowing himself to realize that what he had envisioned had come to be.

It was a brief yet personally significant moment.

A vision, whether it's to build a company, travel the world, or reach the highest level within a profession, is the treasure. The path to the treasure can be through hell or heaven. To realize the vision, requires a never wavering effort. Every step and decision, every opportunity, every challenge, every setback, every moment on the path to achieving your vision requires accepting that everything you do is bringing you closer to what you want.

Many people have a vision, to varying degrees, of something. Many keep it with them all their lives, never pursuing it, never achieving it. Others are obsessed with their vision, going after it at all costs.

Visions have been the salvation for some, the ruin for others.

Your vision may be grandiose or simple. The key is to commit to and link every effort to achieving it.

Your vision may not include being a great communicator, but becoming the best communicator you can be will keep you on a course to realizing your vision. Whether it's small and of the moment, like getting a promotion, or larger, like getting money for your startup, or winning a huge contract for your company, everything rests on your ability to communicate what you want, in a way that convinces your listeners – the bankers, the boss, the client, the governing body – to accept your message.

If your vision is to be a great communicator, good on'ya. If your vision is to be the best (fill in your blank), being a great communicator can be a powerful ally in your quest. A seemingly insignificant conversation can become the catalyst for great change and progress. With everything you communicate, in every environment, with every audience large and small, use the foundations of awareness and empathy to stay on your vision's course.

Vision and communication fuel each other.

I began this book explaining how the end is actually the beginning. Your vision came first; now you're in the journey to realize the vision, that end which you first saw at the beginning.

I told you it would all make sense eventually.

"Five minutes, five minutes to curtain..."

We have made you aware, tapped into traits, philosophies, emotions and practicalities, all of which you may not have, until now, connected to the ways of being a better, effective communicator.

You have learned that effective communication requires looking at yourself and evaluating your message through the perspectives of your audience.

You've learned that every audience, of one or one-thousand, consists of people who want to hear what you have to say.

You've learned that effectively communicating requires not just a connection to the audience, but your own connection to and awareness of your physical and emotional states.

It's time for you to take the stage. But before I send you on your way to Performance, let me leave you with thoughts on passion.

When you have it, you are fueled, you are energized; you will do almost anything when you are passionate about something.

Be passionate as a rule. In your growing awareness of everything around you, in your growing awareness of yourself, of your vision, of your quest to be a better communicator, be passionate about...everything. Many public speaking and presenting coaches stress how important it is to convey your passion to your audience. This is true, but passion isn't something to convey as much as it is something to set free.

Passion comes from within, a natural energy that roils around inside us. The proper way to convey your passion is to get out of passion's way, let it come through on its own. The foundational reason to master public speaking and presenting techniques is so nothing stops the conveyance of passion, honesty and truth flowing from you to your audience. When you master the practical and emotional ways of communication, when you don't have to think about how you're standing, how you look, or what you were supposed to say next, you allow everything that is intrinsic about you to flow from you to the audience.

Learn and master the attributes of great communication, and your passion will flow.

Section Three - Performance

All Eyes are, Indeed, on You

And that's okay; that's what you want. You're the presenter, the meeting's guest speaker, the final interviewee, someone with a story to tell and a venue full of people who want to hear it.

You don't want the audience looking anywhere but at you.

For purposes of The Way to Communicate, performance does not refer to the construction and presentation of a character or persona, or of a talent showcase; it is instead the culmination of a method that when practiced will get you and your head out of your own way.

Much of the content in this section is organized as if you are presenting to a live audience, but, as with prior sections, the guidance works whether you're preparing a speech, having lunch with a client, participating in a seminar or getting ready to face a day of multiple meetings at work. As I have stressed all along, being a compelling, sincere communicator requires integrating more than the mechanics of presentations or presenting yourself well. Effectively communicating requires the understanding and adoption of personal, philosophical, and lifestyle attributes. Embrace The Way to Communicate's methods and you can apply them to any business, professional, and personal communicating situation.

The best method for getting out of your own way, regardless of whether you use nothing else from The Way to Communicate's method, is to work diligently, almost maddeningly, on your presentation, your speech, or those important elements of your impending interview. Prepare, prepare, prepare.

There are actors and entertainers whose work seems so effortless that their performances seem to be personifications of themselves, as opposed to creating characters or performing routines. These perceptions have some merit, but I assure you that few things are as hard as appearing to 'be yourself' while work-ing in a world created from stage directions and lines of dialog, within equipment-laden studios operated by staffs and crews. Yet, when performers are at the top of their game, you accept the creation of their make-believe environment, and they make you feel like you know them.

Performers and creators work hard, continuously, to reach a stage where technique is transparent. One of my favorite writers, Jon Hassler, wrote novels about the everyday lives of people in small Minnesota communities. His writing made me feel as if I was sitting at a small table with the characters, listening to them tell their stories. That feeling of easy intimacy is a hard-won trait that requires constant work (even for someone as talented as Jon).

Work hard in preparation, know your content, go over it and over it and over it, and no matter how you might feel inside, to the outside world – your audience – you'll be remarkably natural and confident.

Professionalism

You don't have to be a professional to have the work ethic of a professional.

Being a professional is a multi-tiered regimen of education, training, practice, and consistency. Someone who drives a truck is not necessarily a professional truck driver, just as someone who works as a security guard or loss prevention specialist is not necessarily a law enforcement professional. Those situations, however, do not preclude people in these positions from applying the traits of a professional to their own situations.

If you imagine yourself as a company, your new awareness and implementation of The Way to Communicate's attributes are your Intellectual Property, your IP. In this final section, we now connect your personal IP to operations and production. Profes-sionals comport themselves as representing the highest levels of their industry, and, therefore, they bring that professional atti-tude into every aspect of their lives, from the way they dress (in professional sports, that extends even to how they get dressed), to the tools they use, to the way they present themselves in public.

There is pride in being known or perceived as a professional.

A professional understands the importance of many everyday things that other people take for granted – being on time, staying on schedule, returning emails and phone calls promptly, dressing well, organizing the day, etc.

Your Performance attributes - awareness, content, empathy, focus

You will rely on all of The Way to Communicate's attributes on your way to the stage, but by spinning your circle of attributes so that awareness, content, empathy, and focus are at the top, you can be assured that they will provide a gateway to all the other attributes during your presentation.

Where did you come from, and how did you get here, moments away from your presentation to the team, your participation on the panel, or your final interview?

It was all in your preparation.

Your preparation began with your assignment, your choice, your appointment, or your mandate. You began with notes and research, progressed to an outline, and developed your presentation with your partners, staff or co-presenters.

From the beginning, you knew who the audience would be, and what they were expecting to see and hear. You knew where you would present and in what kind of environment.

You conferred with the person who knows the AV requirements.

You travelled, arrived, and you are now...

In The Wings

The wings are the areas offstage, right and left, where actors exit and enter scenes, where the stage manager and crews work backstage magic.

Metaphorically, as you enter the room, hall or office where you will eventually present, you are in the wings of your communication situation.

You're ready to go, because you have...

An organized, well-designed, compelling presentation, speech, or social interaction plan

Never wing it.

Casual conversations notwithstanding, I'm insisting that you should never go into any presentation or communication situation with the audacity and egotistical approach of, "I'll just wing it."

It's disrespectful to your audience, disrespectful to yourself, and even if it occasionally works successfully, you are always thisclose to dropping out of the sky instead of soaring above the clouds. It only takes a thought along the lines of "Wait, where the hell was I going with this point?" or an "Omigosh, I forgot to thank the division manager!" and you'll be watching the wings fall off your high-flying sense of self.

There's no reason to wing anything.

Be prepared.

Preparation includes an organized, well-designed, compelling presentation, speech, or social interaction plan.

Wait, wait, what's a social interaction plan?

Not every communication situation is a presentation or speech. Industry-sponsored soirées, social networking events, job interview situations, luncheons and fundraising events aren't presentation venues, per se, but even these more-social-than-business environments can be great communication opportunities. You can plan for these social communication situations more effectively by reviewing what the networking event or environment is about, planning for who might be there and who will be there, and organizing your thoughts as to the kind of conversations you might have with people you know and don't know.

Under normal circumstances, blatant promotion of yourself and your cause at professional networking or professional social events are NOT smart strategies; these ARE, however, opportunities for you to provide people with a sense of who you are, what you do, and what matters to you. This doesn't mean you can't have fun, or that you constantly have to work the room, but keep a sense of why you're there, why you wanted to be there, or why you were asked to attend.

Regardless of what it is – social interaction, speech, presentation, interview, sales call – the reward for familiarity with your content is freedom: freedom from worry, freedom from mistakes, and, on the chance that there might be a mistake (because that's life), freedom to get back on track.

One of the most underused techniques for insuring the success of your presentation is rehearsal.

Rehearsal is NOT sitting at your desk and clicking through all your slides on your monitor, and it's not doing it with a projector in a conference room...but at least that's closer. Rehearsal is DOING your presentation, standing at the front of a room, reading from your notes, moving through your slides, and making the same kind of energetic, enthusiastic effort you will use for the real thing. Even a willing audience of one helps. Your pacing, emphasis, even the order of your slides, can all benefit from a 'real' rehearsal. Videotaping yourself is also a smart move, because no matter how we believe we look, move and sound, our self-perception rarely matches reality.

Before we actually walk the path that takes you from the wings to center stage for your performance, I'm going to present some mechanical information, the basics, dos-and-don'ts, should haves and shouldn't haves, of formats, technologies, and you. Although for simplicity's sake I refer to your 'presentation' in most of what follows, the guidance relates to any kind of important communications situation, from a designer's portfolio review to a CEO's keynote.

A reminder: Whether it's a speech or presentation, stick with three acts.

Three good acts: start a story, tell a story, end a story.

At the beginning of this book, I explained how our lives are mini three-act stories strung together: coming from somewhere, being somewhere, going somewhere. If you've written speeches or you've had education or training on "how to write", you're probably familiar with the three-act process. If most of the writing you do, however, is within the context of presentations, you may not realize that the beginning/middle/end structure is still important.

I don't know the origin of the "tell them what you're going to tell them, tell them, and tell them what you told them" advice, but it is a simplified business version of the three-act structure.

Your three-act structure is what you adhere to from the earliest stages of your presentation's development. It's not something that can be added to your presentation or public appearance as you're walking to the podium, although there have been and always will be those who attempt to do just that.

Here's an easy to remember guide for constructing a three-act presentation:

Overture - Decide what you want the audience to remember when the presentation is over: "We're number one!"

Act One – State your case: We're number one!

Act Two – Make your case: Here's how we've won everything there ever was.

Act Three – Close your case: We're number one; we know it; we've proven it; now you know it.

Here's another important presentation rule to live by: if your slides have more than two bullet points per slide, a smattering of clip art, graphs and charts in their raw format, no pictures, and no pictures of PEOPLE, you need to rework your presentation. Imagine your audience's perspective and you should be able to envision why: you at the front of the room, reading your bullet points aloud, the audience occasionally reading the bullet points – or, more likely, trying to read your bullet points – ignoring the clip art, and, with no images to connect to, the audience wonders, "How much longer before this is all over?"

That is not the way to communicate.

One of the common yet serious missteps in any presentation is to not have a single picture of a human being anywhere in the presentation. As the reigning intelligent species on the planet, one of the automatic things we're predisposed to do is to recognize and LOOK at other human beings. Unlike other animal species that interpret most eyeball to eyeball contact as a threat, we look at each other, and that means that a presentation which includes images of people is looked at and accepted far more than one without.

Have mercy on your audience and give them a presentation that actually has a chance to connect with them.

Some mechanics: formats and redundancy
Paper and fonts

With all the advantages and whizz-bang possibilities of audio/visual systems, it only takes a moment for a cable to be tripped over, a circuit breaker to pop, or an operating system to crash. With a printed copy of your presentation, you can at least do a version of your presentation if there's an equipment problem. If you're in an interview or on a sales call, and animations, video, diagrams or artwork were your aces in the hole, you may still win if you at least have printed screen captures. In many instances, you may actually find it easier and more dynamic to use both.

Paper never goes down, never freezes, doesn't erase itself, never has to be plugged in, and, as long as it's in its owner's possession, it doesn't require much of a search to find it.

If you're a Powerpoint user, you are probably aware of how to use the Notes mode of your presentation (we'll get to the Speaker Mode of Powerpoint in a bit). Whether you print out your Powerpoint Notes to use for a presentation or you're in a scripted situation, such as leading a panel or being the master of ceremonies for an event, there are several very helpful formatting and preparation techniques which you should always use:

Use a large, san serif font that you can read beyond arm's length (try 14 or 16 point as a start), the approximate distance from your eyes to the top of a podium. (a san serif font is one without the extended, flat parts at the top and bottom of the letters; Arial is sans serif; Times New Roman is serif)

Don't use all uppercase; it's very hard to read.

Use a yellow highlighter to indicate where you can lift your eyes from the script to look at the audience. The highlighted area is very easy to see and serves to both remind you to look up and to easily find your place in the script when you look back down. You can also rest a finger next to the highlighted area to make it even easier to keep your place. (If you are a more experienced speaker or presenter, you may already know that moving around the stage instead of staying at the podium is a very favorable approach; highlighted areas of text make it easier to find your way around your outline when you move back to the podium.)

Each script page should end with a complete sentence. As you speak, turn the page just before you reach the end of the sentence. This gives you a smooth speaking transition.

If you're working from a script, you don't want to wait – if at all possible – until the day of the presentation or event to see the final version. Many scripted events have a scheduled rehearsal or technical run thru, and the script you receive for the run thru should be the final version. You'll need a pen to make notes and indications of everything from notations to yourself ("pause here; point to Mr. Smith – he'll be seated in the first row, middle") to music cues and things you couldn't possibly have known until now ("extra time for Ms. Jones to reach the stage.") – and make sure you write large enough, and neatly enough, to read easily.

Whether you use a printed or onscreen version of Notes, you can use the formatting menu to adjust the font size and highlight the text.

Many users are still not aware of Presenter Mode in Powerpoint. This is a great interface for presentations. It shows the slide that is currently on the screen; the next slide; a small column of all the slides in the presentation (which are clickable, allowing the presenter to select any slide at any time during the presentation); and the Notes or text of the presentation. Your computer must be in two-monitor mode to access Presenter Mode (two-monitor mode works when a laptop is connected to a projector).

A very special note to you

Whether you've written every word you're going to utter or you've put together a fairly concise outline, always write out the first three sentences you are going to say. Memorize them if that's easy for you to do, but make sure that the first three lines of your notes, outline, script, whatever, are the first three things you say out loud. It may sound trite or simplistic but, like some of the other effective mental programming techniques I've described, this one works to ease that first-words-out-of-your-mouth tension, makes it easy for you to start, and prevents you from saying something less than appropriate (which has been the downfall of many presenters who changed the opening of their speech because they had a last minute idea that they felt was funny, pithy or relevant, but once uttered was none of those).

Redundancy and equipment

Have a nicely formatted, printed version of your presentation. Put it in a slim binder, which you'll take to the podium with you. If you feel that a binder isn't right for the presentation, then paperclip the pages together and leave them clipped until you do your presentation.

Have digital backups of your presentation (or resume', or sales demo, etc.), from the more reliable to least desirable, on an external USB or Firewire drive, a DVD or CD, a thumb drive.

Thumb drives can be unreliable and are easiest to lose, but they do have the same advantage as an external drive: if you make changes (necessary changes, not the willy-nilly kind) to the master presentation, you can back it up easily. Backup is still possible with rewritable DVDs and CDs, but the rewriting and burning process requires more time, with more potential for technical problems.

Many conferences and seminars request that presentations be submitted prior to the event. For these situations, have a backup that matches the original format requirements (for example, "submissions on DVD-RW are acceptable -- we cannot use DVD+RW"; this is an unlikely requirement, but not unheard of).

Keep a pocket-sized notepad or notebook, and pen or pencil with you all the time. The world doesn't stop turning, things change constantly, and you just never know what you'll have to remind yourself of and keep track of right up to the moment of your presentation: jotting down some names of people who you want to mention; additional statistics; thoughts or news items.

If you're going to use:

A laptop or other portable device, make sure the battery is fully charged (have a spare with you, if feasible);

A pen, use a new one with plenty of ink; mechanical pencil, plenty of lead;

A projector - set it up well before you need it (including the laptop or device that has the presentation), and know how to access and use the projector's menu.

Be aware and know how to deal with a projector and laptop that go to screensaver, power save or hibernation modes. This is especially important because once a projector or its connected laptop go into any of those modes, it may take up to a minute or more for everything to wake up...and a minute of vamp time at the start of a presentation is not a good thing (it will feel like a lifetime).

Internet access during a presentation: it's ALWAYS better to save any web pages and web animations to your hard drive. Don't rely on having Net access at your event, even if it's been promised. The reasons are legion, starting with the drawbacks of using and relying upon Internet-based resources accessed through someone else's network. For example, a site you need to access as part of your sales call might be blocked by your customer's finicky firewall.

Organize, charge, gather and pack your equipment and presentation-related material long before you have to leave for the venue. This should include any documentation, show registration, passes, tickets, directions to the event, and anything else you need to get to and into wherever you're going. Doing this the night before is best.

Know as much about the event personnel as possible: names and cell phone numbers for people in your company and those staff and crew connected to the venue, where they can be found at what times, etc.

Know how you're going to get to where you need to be, and verify the arrangements.

Have a fallback plan ready if, despite your stellar efforts on the above, the taxi or van you reserved simply doesn't show up.

Before you walk out of your room or office, make sure you've got everything you need, and walk around to verify that you do (this is called an idiot check; I'll go into detail about it in a few pages).

All of this serves a very important purpose: it removes degrees of worry and anxiety, and when worry and anxiety are lessened, relaxation, focus and concentration are increased.

Preparing you, personally

Don't overdo anything the night before the presentation. Don't: overeat; drink to excess; blow out your voice the night before by trying to converse in a club playing music at high volume; stay awake long after your usual bedtime; rewrite your entire presentation; or...

Rather than put a long list together, let the following tale be of guidance.

Be Normal -- Why, when, and how to stick with the things that got you there

Normal is different for everyone. I shall never fully understand why some people choose to deviate from whatever normal is for them just when normal is what they need most. This was clearly the case when Maureen Merrill, the principal of Harris-Merrill Consulting, asked me to assist her with a client preparing for an appearance on a nationally broadcast, morning television show.

The work of her client's successful nonprofit was well-regarded, and its programs appealed to a wide demographic.

The client had made many TV appearances over the years, and had told the nonprofit's story so many times that story fatigue had set in. It no longer seemed fresh or exciting, and the client began to worry about sounding egotistical. The client wanted to change how the story was presented, but couldn't find a way to do that without being at the center of the story.

This isn't an unusual situation. Story fatigue and the "I sound like I'm always talking about myself" feeling can be a natural result when people who formed an organization, and remain vested in the organization's success, are also the best choice to be its spokesperson.

Story fatigue is remedied by identifying what the story is and isn't.

If the storyteller is the very reason the organization exists (to varying degrees, this is often the case), the storyteller can consider himself or herself as the organization's mobile museum.

The storyteller becomes the carrier of the story, and he or she just happens to be an integral part of it. Acceptance of this as objectively true is the first step to removing the storyteller's ego, their sense of self, from the story. An effective mental exercise to support this approach is to have the founder or creator of the organization imagine being in the audience as the story is told. It gives the speaker a perspective from which he or she can hear the story.

Next, the storyteller has to accept that the story is always new to those who haven't heard it. As story fatigue develops, the storyteller increasingly feels that he is talking about himself, even though he always tells the same story. The storyteller loses focus on the purpose of the story, which is to share it with an audience. When a storyteller focuses on himself – "I bet I look great up here," or "I suck right now" – the teller's and the story's impact are diminished.

Realigning the spokesperson's objectiveness about the story and its purpose should re-energize the storyteller.

This resonated with Maureen's client, and helped the client regain some of the natural enthusiasm for the nonprofit's work. We also reviewed what to do the morning of the show. Earlier, the client had made some passing remarks about breakfast and coffee. I thought it was a good idea to review the Twenty-Minutes-to-Curtain Dos and Don'ts: no cold fluids (tightens the vocal cords), room temperature water is best, etc. (a complete Dos and Don'ts list is on The Way to Communicate's website). I also stressed the importance of the client's normal morning routine.

Although coffee might be part of the morning routine, it is a bit of an upper, and it could affect or intensify any nervousness before a show. I suggested drinking only half of the usual amount of morning coffee, and having the remainder after the appearance.

"Oh," the client said, "I don't drink coffee."

"But, didn't you say you'd have coffee that morning?"

"Yes, but I only drink coffee whenever I do an appearance or give a talk."

I truly hoped I didn't look as perplexed as I felt. "You don't usually drink coffee? How much do you have before an appearance, usually?"

"Two big cups. I figure it'll give me energy."

I wanted to say, yes, it will, like a Super Ball ricocheting around a concrete room. But I held back, and Maureen and I explained, in our best professional manner and using different words than I use here, why that really wasn't a good idea.

The client agreed.

Normal is best. Everything about The Way to Communicate method needs to be learned, practiced and used, but when everything comes together its end result is to make it easiest for you to be 'you', an effective presenter.

So, with a few minor alterations, the best way to prep for a presentation is to do the normal things you do on any normal day. From the clothes you wear to the meals you eat, don't do anything that you've never done before.

On the day you're going to present, don't have hot sauce on your eggs if you've never had eggs prepared that way. Don't wear a pair of shoes that you've never worn or only worn once (and consider having a pair of shoes with different soles as a backup; I once watched a well-regarded, tall business woman take tiny, Hobbit-like steps across a banquet room, the leather soles of her fashionable high heels unable to maintain traction on the carpet).

You can, and should, be yourself for any appearance. Your preparation, message and personal presentation skills won't help you if you've gone and done something goofy and gotten in your own way. Just be yourself; be normal.

You're on location

Arrive at your destination with plenty of time to do your awareness checks on yourself and your environment.

You've dressed appropriately and comfortably, and you have your materials. As you arrive and move to the room, hall or other specific location for your presentation, look around, feel the energy around you. Depending on the timing and logistics, you may want to go right to your presentation's location and, if the area is secure, drop off your gear and go to the room where you'll be presenting. This may not be possible if you're attending a meeting in a place of business other than your own, doing a sales call, or going to a job interview.

In those situations that don't allow for arriving early and checking out the environment, arrive as early as acceptable. Remember your awareness checks. If you need to set up a projector or other equipment, ask your contact at the location to allow you into the room or space as soon as convenient.

Check in with the A/V person or your contact to verify that everything is ready, and that the setup and equipment is what you require. This is very important, because equipment substitutions, room changes, schedules, and miscommunications happen all the time! The earlier you know about an alteration of your expectations the easier it is to adapt.

Go sit, stand, and walk around in the area where you will work. You may have to ask permission to do this. If the room is occupied – multiple seminars or training sessions, for example – coordinate an opportunity to access the room and the presentation area between sessions.

If you have questions about anything pertaining to the area where you will work, about the equipment, the condition of the room, ask! ("Can we dim the room lights, or can we at least turn off all but a few?" is one of those questions that should have been asked ahead of time). Be professional, courteous, and if things aren't setup as was represented, attempt to make them right. You may have to balance the effort and time necessary to retool the area (from yours and the event staff's perspectives) against working with what you have; only you will be able to make that decision.

If you supplied an advanced copy of your presentation, check with your contact to insure they have it, and that what they believe are your materials are, indeed, yours.

Check the schedule – remember, things do change – and if everything seems to be in place, take a few moments to relax and breathe. Or get to work, because your talk, presentation or interview may not be your only commitment for that day. The downside of all this concentration on preparing and delivering a great presentation is that it's probably not the only thing you do in your job.

"Places, everyone..."

Be on time, in your chair on the dais, at the side of the stage, in your seat in the audience, at your company's trade show booth, in the reception area...be there.

Adhering to the schedule contributes to the smooth functioning of the show, and, frankly, you will have the (often unsaid) appreciation of the people actually running the show. That, in turn, can be of great benefit if you need assistance or have a request.

Whether the waiting area is offstage or you're seated at the dais, have your materials ready. And, whether you're offstage or at the dais, you can skim your script or speech, but there's no hope that you'll suddenly learn and absorb anything you don't already know. This is another reason why it is so important to know your material. The time between when you arrive and when you have to speak may collapse at frightening speed, filled with greetings, conversations, or last minute, urgent situations that must be dealt with.

When you do have time and you are in a waiting area away from the audience's view, review your material, but be aware of what's happening. The speaker before you may make a reference or say something that you could make a remark about during your presentation, or a technical situation may crop up, such as a bad microphone, flickering lights, etc. You'll benefit greatly by being aware of and ready for such unplanned challenges.

In a dais situation, it appears rude if you're seen studiously reviewing your own material while another panel member is presenting or speaking. It is, however, acceptable and recommended to make notes.

Your moments in the wings, or just before you take your seat on the panel, or walk into the room for your sales call or interview, is your last opportunity to do a personal idiot check, a concept I picked up as a roadie. Roadies, like salespeople and other mobile professionals, spend an ungodly amount of time in hotels, and the last thing a roadie does when checking out of a hotel room (a smart roadie, that is) is an idiot check. A walk around the room, checking every nook and cranny, to verify that everything has been packed and nothing has been left behind.

The hook on the back of a bathroom door has been the cause of many a left behind article of clothing. A roadie learns it early in his or her career, and it probably derived from someone who uttered, "man, I am such an idiot" after realizing a few hours later, and a few hundred miles away, that something important had been left behind.

The personal idiot check is very simple (best done with a mirror, but if one isn't available, ask someone to look you over):
Zipper up? Men's pants, women's pants, skirts, and dresses.
Hair okay? No weird cowlicks, overturned comb-overs, or foreign matter.
Any stains on you pants, shirt, or tie?
Wearing a matching pair of shoes?
Tie or other accessory straight?
Anything anywhere on your face or teeth that shouldn't be there?
Show pass, ID, or accreditation documents in your possession?
Cell phone off?

So now, with minutes to go...you wait
While you wait:
Don't eat right up to the time you have to present or give your talk. At breakfast, lunch or dinner functions, stop eating twenty-minutes before your presentation. Stop drinking coffee or tea ten minutes before your time. The best liquid as you wait is cool, not cold, water. Most catered events provide as much water as you wish, but it's almost always ice water. You can ask for a glass or pitcher of water without ice, but you're best served by bringing your own small bottle of water with you.

If you or your organization is putting on the event, or you're appearing at an event where you have some input, request pitchers of water without ice. Nothing is louder amidst an otherwise quiet and attentive audience than the clatter of ice cubes rattling around a pitcher as someone fills a glass...and someone always fills a glass as you speak.

Those pesky ol' nerves

As the minutes wind down to your time in the spotlight, you may discover that despite your best efforts to follow and adopt all the guidance on these pages, you still feel a tightness in your stomach, the room suddenly feels warm, and your heart rate is creeping up.

It's okay. You're going to be fine.

You can alleviate some of what you feel by first exhaling, then taking in some air in a longer than usual, controlled manner. Pull back your shoulders slightly to open your chest, and sit up straight. Exhale, and as you do, release the tension in your shoulders. You probably weren't aware that you were holding your shoulders up, as if at the top of a shrug. Take another deep breath, deep into your lower lungs, breathe out in your normal manner, and drink some water.

As your anxiety began increasing, your breathing probably became shallower. The first exhale both blows out the carbon dioxide and resets your respiratory rate. The next couple of controlled breaths should start to bring down your heart rate and help you resume a normal breathing pattern. That, in turn, will benefit everything by bringing oxygen into your system and clearing your head.

As you begin to feel more in control, turn your focus to the speaker or presentation, which will help you take your mind off yourself.

You'll be fine.

It's no secret that many people who make their livelihoods in front of audiences still feel some touch of anxiety just before they go on, and most of them are okay with that. A touch of nerves in these situations is closer to normal than you might at first assume. While a few people may overcome their fears and anxieties completely, most do what you will eventually do - rather than totally overcome their anxiety, they manage it.

Fear is a legitimate emotion with physical manifestations, but with focus and concentration, people can learn to function and work through their fear or anxiety. To help you establish control over your feelings in the last moments before you go on, here's a powerful, effective mental tool: the Switch.

Throwing the Switch

In athletics, it's known as putting on your game face; some performers call it taking a moment.

For communicators, I call it the Switch.

I recounted in Being Normal the tale from my work with consultant Maureen Merrill. She provides coaching on an ongoing basis to a group of professionals who normally are large and in charge, who dive into, establish and maintain control of chaotic, intense, dangerous situations: police officers.

These men and women come for help with one of the few situations that seems to suck varying degrees of confidence out of them: appearing in front of a promotions board and responding orally to questions. They must enter a room, in 'normal' clothes, sit across a table from several of their superiors, answer questions and make succinct statements, the content of which will, in combination with other attributes, either further their career or delay their promotion.

No patrol car, no belt laden with the tools of the profession, no uniform, none of the physicality, street psychology or the cachet that those tools and their appearance provide on the beat. The promotions board environment is almost totally alien to police officers, physically and mentally.

Coaching helps them adjust to the environment and present themselves as being worthy and capable. Their story is relevant because it's an example of how professionals with the skill and training to handle the most stressful situations can make themselves feel vulnerable and insecure when taken out of their comfort zone.

I use techniques of The Way to Communicate method to work on their physical and mental states, and train them to use the Switch.

I began Section Two, Run Thru, with "Get ready for the real thing, because you're going to have to do it anyway"; the Switch is the key to being ready.

In Young Frankenstein, the great Mel Brooks film starring Gene Wilder, there's a pivotal scene wherein Dr. Frankenstein is poised to bring his creature to life. Amidst the din of a thunderstorm, Frankenstein commands Igor, his bug-eyed, hunchbacked assistant, to throw the first switch, then the second switch, then, to throw the all-important "big' switch". As the film cuts to actor Marty Feldman's character, he places his hands on a large switch, next to but much larger than the previous two switches. Appropriately for a Mel Brooks comedy, it is labeled The Big Switch.

"Are you sure, master?"

"Yes!"

It's a great comedic example of a pivotal moment, where moving forward is the commitment – there will be no going back.

Pick an analogy: stepping off the cliff to take that forty-foot drop into the swimming hole; pushing off for your first run down an advanced slope; telling the boss you're quitting; saying your first words into the microphone as the applause dies down.

There's no going back; that's what Dr. Frankenstein is accepting as he tells Igor to throw the switch.

Athletes across the spectrum of sports have all sorts of routines they use as their Switch. During one summer Olympics, it was clearly evident that in the last moments before a particular sprinter took a position in the blocks, she had a routine of touching the ring on her finger, in a very specific way, then touching a chain around her neck.

From that moment, there was nothing else in existence accept the race; her race.

Your Switch is that moment when you place yourself in a mental state of concentrated focus. Whether going into an interview, walking up to the podium, or standing at the head of a long conference table, when you throw the Switch your focus is on the continuous string of moments from just before to the end of your performance.

It begins when you receive your cue:

"Come on in, Mr. Adams."

"It's my pleasure to present Sylvia Sarah."

"All right, Fred, let's hear your report."

The moment you hear it, you turn on your Switch. The Switch needs to be personal and uncomplicated: an image, phrase or word. It has to be more than a random thought. Your Switch is an internal command, a call to your personal processing center that initiates a specific action. Your Switch is a specific call to your processing center that says, "Go communicate."

It can be words or images: here we go; let's rock; go; I'm on; all right; mazeltoff; a light switch; a traffic light; you throwing a football; opening a door.

Surprisingly, without realizing it, you will almost certainly abandon the Switch at some point in your communicating life. The Switch clears your mind in the critical last moments before you begin your presentation. At some point you will eventually realize that you have been beginning your presentations without it, because after a certain number of repetitions, your brain will move into a level of concentration on its own, without throwing the Switch.

You'll always have it whenever you have difficulty focusing. But, the Switch's greatest benefit may very well be that it realizes before you do that it's no longer needed, and turns itself off.

And, you're on

Watch where you're going as you walk to the podium, into the room, or to center stage.

If you weren't part of the set-up or technical rehearsal for an event or large-scale presentation, and especially if the event is being videotaped or broadcast, you may be surprised at the brightness of the lights. They can be so distracting you might not see cords, cables, steps, or the legs of chairs.

Personally thank the person who just introduced you, but don't do it into the microphone, yet, and thank that person again, into the microphone, as you begin your presentation. Normally, there's no reason you wouldn't acknowledge your introducer. If you're wearing a lav mic – a small, wireless microphone that attaches to a lapel or shirt – the sound tech will probably have made your mic live as you were introduced (or 'hot', the technical term). Keep this in mind, and speak in a normal but soft voice as you say anything prior to the actual start of your presentation.

Sound techs usually attach lav microphones long before the presentation itself begins. The mic is sometimes powered on, but muted at the sound board. When you have to power on your own microphone, the tech will show you how, and you shouldn't power it on until you've been introduced.

The number one rule when wearing or in the range of any microphone: NEVER say anything that you wouldn't want the entire world to hear. History is replete with open microphone gaffs. Don't join the list.

Resist touching or adjusting the podium microphone.

Place your materials on the podium. Glance at the projector screen, your laptop screen, and at the first page of your speech or script. If your first slide is not on the screen, advance to it. This really takes no more than a few seconds, about the time it takes for applause to wind down.

Now, set yourself physically; whether you are at a podium or on a bare stage, begin by placing your feet at least shoulder-width apart. Many people have a tendency to shift their weight as they speak, or, if moving around, have a tendency to adopt odd postures and stances of which they're not even aware. If you're at the podium, plant your feet but don't lock your knees, and let yourself move and turn when you have to. If you feel the need for a bit more security, go ahead and lightly grip the sides of the podium. Don't make it a death grip, and at some point, let go and allow your arms and hands to move freely.

Tiny, slight changes in posture, like shifting from one leg to the other, leaning this way and that, are magnified and obvious when you are the focus of everyone's attention. A balanced stance at the podium is best for you and your audience.

If you feel more comfortable when you're not constrained by a podium, that's great, but be aware of how you appear when you stand still or pause. When you're not moving, you should be comfortably balanced. If you're stepping sideways, and you stop as you emphasize something, make sure you haven't stopped with your legs crossed. It happens to presenters more than you might realize, and it can make you look like you need to hit the restroom. If you do realize you've adopted that position -- usually because you see someone in the audience look at your legs – simply step out of it and resume a 'normal' stance.

Look out to the audience. If there are people you know seated in the first few rows, give them a smile or nod of recognition.

Before you open your mouth

I don't know where or how it started. It may even be that it comes from something in our primal brain, a deep-seated reaction held over from when presentations were given around the campfire and dinosaurs attempted to eat the audience. Perhaps it's because it looks like a snake that should be grabbed just behind the head so it can't strike. Whatever the reason, so many people do it that I must at least try to stop it before the next sound tech runs screaming from the auditorium.

There are a few exceptions of which I'll get to momentarily, but, as a general rule, DON'T TOUCH THE PODIUM MICROPHONE, please, unless the sound tech says it's all right, and he'll appreciate that you asked. It happens so often that I may be the last of those hoping for a tidal change.

The typical podium mic is a small, sponge-covered ball at the end of a gooseneck mic holder, that thing that rises up from the podium like a thin snake. Podium mics have an audio pickup range that enables them to transmit a speaker's voice without the speaker having to appear as if they've thrown their back out.

There are times that a readjustment of the mic's position is required. If one presenter is six-two, and the next is five-two, yes, an adjustment must be made. But for the majority of situations, if the little ball at the end of the gooseneck seems to be pointed at your face, you're probably fine.

It's unusual but not unheard of that a handheld microphone has to be used at a podium. Often, a handheld mic is placed on the podium's inside shelf as a backup in case the podium mic goes down. Handheld microphones, now almost always wireless, are used for presenters who move around the stage, but they have lost favor with many professional speakers and presenters who now use the wireless lav, or the almost invisible, wireless headset which rests on the ear and has a thin, powerful mic that extends along the side of the cheek.

Presenters unfamiliar with handheld mics, and even many

experienced users, bedevil both sound techs and audiences. Know this: how close the mic is held to your mouth is often not as important as the angle of the mic relative to your mouth.

The common misconception is that closer is always better, and this is half-accurate. Many of us have strained to hear someone as they unknowingly drop the mic toward their chest. Someone in the audience shouts "louder", so the speaker quickly brings the mic up to just below the chin, but holds it vertical, parallel to their chest. This makes things better, but it's not the solution.

To utilize the full power of a handheld mic, and put a smile on the sound tech's face, you want to speak into the top of the microphone. Close is good, but close and speaking 'at' the top of the mic is best. Instead of holding the mic straight up and down, parallel to your chest, hold the mic so the top is level with and a couple of inches out from your lips, then push the bottom of the mic away from you by several inches, leaving the top – the North Pole of the mic – still close to your mouth. If you ever used a microphone that was still in its mic stand, or taken notice of microphone placement on a stage or at a concert, you can see that the microphone is generally at the same angle as if you were bringing a bottle or glass to your lips to take a drink.

It's time to release your voice. You're balanced, ready to go. The last thing you do before you speak is take in a breath, so you have some fuel as you begin, and, as you exhale, begin saying your three opening lines.

Being in it - Awareness, content, focus, empathy, and the continuity of each moment

Almost everyone begins with a normal salutation, followed by a statement of what the presentation is about. Many speech coaches prefer that a speaker begin with something different, an anecdote, or event-relevant remark, something that quickly elevates the presentation and the presenter above the standard, "I'm so pleased to be here today..."

I believe "good morning everyone" and similar less-than-fireworks openings are fine, but they should never be followed with "this morning, I'm going to speak about" because everyone in the audience knows why they are there. There are those presenters who can't feel comfortable, however, unless they can 'say' what the presentation is about. If you're in that group, work the title into your opening lines: "We know that customer relationship management programs are the fastest growing segment of our market, but what does that mean for you?"

However you begin, make it something that helps you to feel confident and in control. Don't overwrite your opening. Remember the Be Normal story from a few pages back. Don't use flowery words, overly technical jargon, or obtuse language – be you.

Take your time, begin with your three sentences, and look at your audience. If the person who introduced you is present, look at them, and look anyone else you acknowledge.

Look around the room. For the rest or your performance, balance awareness of your environment with controlled delivery of your message. If the situation is more intimate - a sales call with a few people in attendance - the balance remains the same: awareness of your environment and delivery of your message.

I know that some of you feel nervous right now just reading about presenting.

You'll be all right. Getting started is the fright and the relief. You may feel the nerves right through your first three sentences, but it will subside. The mere act of beginning brings the first release of the anxiety and tension. It provides you with a smooth start, and while you may feel slightly jumbled inside, the smooth start provides you valuable self-feedback: you are in control.

This approach really helps in an interview or smaller interaction setting. Although you may not have the ability to begin the dialog, there will be certain openings for which you can prepare a response:

"Tell us something about yourself."

"You know what we're looking for; tell us how you're going to fix our situation."

"Why do you want to work here?"

Monitor your own sound level as you speak; the longer we speak, the more we drift down in volume, so periodically check in with yourself. If you've been told or you know that you tend to speak softer as you go on, put the word "volume" in the margins or throughout your outline. If you're using a handheld mic, remember to keep it from dropping to our chest, and to hold it as if you were about to take a drink from a glass.

What NOT to say, microphone or not:

"I mean, (followed by anything)..."

"Um..."

"Uh..."

Beginning a statement with "I mean", "So", "I'm all", or inserting "um" and "uh" vocal pauses into your speech may be barely noticeable in general conversation, but will become distracting quickly in speeches and presentations. The use of "I mean" has become so prevalent in American vernacular that I've heard it used by people who speak English as a second language. Prevalence does not validate its use. "I mean" is bereft of substance.

The "um" and "uh" vocal pauses have been with us for eons, and will never go away. Again, though, that doesn't justify their use. It's a habit for most us, but it can be easily unlearned with awareness and effort. It's a nervous habit for some, a crutch to maintain the floor, so to speak, for others. And there are those who can't get comfortable with silence, to the point that someone in a group that has gone quiet for more than a few seconds will say something simply to fill the space.

In a presentation, speech or sales call, you may be tempted to fill in what you feel is an ungodly long period of silence, during a slide transition that doesn't load quickly, for example. Let it ride for the moment, but if you feel that something must be said, go with "well, it was there when I checked this morning" or other brief remark.

Don't be rattled by the silence of a pause; it's okay, and much less distracting than "Umm...umm...uh."

Three sentences down, the rest of the presentation to go

Great presenters know their presentation, script or speech. They may occasionally refer to notes or the script, but they have it memorized, like an actor's lines. The greatest value of committing your content to memory is that it frees you. When you know every word of your presentation you can relax, and when you relax you present your best self to your audience.

Knowing your content allows you to move, to breathe, to emphasize, point, pause, shout, and speak in your most natural, emotional way. It doesn't mean that a presenter must scream, cry or turn cartwheels, unless that is genuinely how that person acts in any situation. An emotional outburst of enthusiasm can still be effective even if it's subtle.

Steve Jobs is not one to go crazy onstage, even as his rapt audience does, indeed, go nuts. But when he says "and it screams" in describing Apple's newest gizmo, he says it with enough Steve Jobs emphasis that everyone knows he believes it.

If you don't believe you, your audience won't believe you either.

Never manufacture emotion; never attempt to force an emotion when it's not what you feel.

There are means and methods you can use to find an emotion to go along with a moment, but it shouldn't be necessary if you understand what you are saying, and understand why what you're saying matters to you. If that sounds simplistic, if not slightly confusing, what follows is an example that demonstrates manufactured emotion, and a lack of awareness.

Several hundred members of an organization had gathered to hear an executive deliver a pivotal speech about the organization's programs. Fifty of the attendees were to be recognized at the program's conclusion.

The executive was an adequate public speaker, but had worked diligently with a consultant and had improved, although some fundamental weaknesses remained.

During the speech, I overheard someone in the audience quietly say that the executive frowned too much.

It was an accurate but sad observation, because the executive was actually attempting to convey a sense of seriousness, of genuine concern.

Over the course of the previous month, the consultant had drawn attention to certain statements in the speech that were not just important, but would also really connect with the audience. The consultant had pointed out "this line here, what you're saying here, this is so strong, it really sums up why this program makes a difference..."

The result, though, was that the executive couldn't seem to understand that the truth of the statement didn't need to be emphasized, it instead needed to be said from the heart.

Because the executive didn't grasp the difference between saying something in a meaningful fashion and saying something meaningful, the executive attempted to convey an emotion, instead of believing in the truth of what was being said. The executive was focused on sounding and looking like "I care", but the result was a distraction.

The executive never really did connect with the heart of the speech, and was so concerned about portraying concern, that when it was time to talk about those who were to be recognized, the executive spoke to them, complimenting them, without realizing they had all had quietly left the room a few minutes earlier to assemble in the outside hall. And the executive stayed unaware of their absence until they filed back into the room, on cue, at the end of the speech.

By focusing solely on what was supposed to be conveyed, and never connecting the words of the speech to the emotions of what those words meant, the speaker presented a string of awkward moments.

Later that evening, another speaker came to the podium, unfolded several sheets of paper and told a personal story of obstacles overcome and achievements gained. She barely looked up as she read, and her delivery was far from polished, but at the end there wasn't a dry eye in the hall. She infused her story with truth, unconcerned about how to say things, delivering words shaped and colored by her heart.

Most of our presentations and speeches have little to do with our personal lives, but every story should convey our convictions.

How well you deliver your message and how effective you are as a communicator depends on your ability to connect your content to your audience. You are the interface, the portal, the human connection between the content on the slide or in your speech, facilitating delivery of the content into the hearts and minds of your audience.

You are the content.

Ask ten artists to paint a portrait of the same model, and you get ten radically different paintings. The variations will be exponential: thick strokes of paint; thin strokes; bold colors; subdued colors; composition; on canvas; on paper; realistic; abstract. The choices reflect unique styles and tools, and the final results funnel down to emotions: how does the portrait make you feel?

Your content is what it is, but how you present it and how you offer it are keys to how your audience feels about it and about you.

As you present, your audience will slowly merge you and your message. They will occasionally read the text on your slide and look at the pictures, but their eyes and attention will always return to you.

As you and your content merge, don't allow yourself to dis' your audience. Make every effort to not turn your back to them. Every time you turn your face away from your audience, they can't hear you. Turn slightly and glance over your shoulder at a projected slide, but turn back to face your audience. Even better, go and actually stand next to or in front of your projected slides, or interact with them (like a TV meteorologist). Yes, you may have to turn your back to get to the screen, but this is different than standing at a podium, turning away from your audience and reading your slide aloud (and, if you're reading your slide aloud, I must remind you about not having a list of bullets on your slide in the first place).

About laser pointers: don't use them. I would much rather see someone walk to their projected slide and point to something than have to find the little, jiggling dot on the screen. Presenters believe it 'helps' the audience. It may, I guess, but if you feel the need to point out something specific on the slide with a laser pointer, then you should redesign your slide so that what you believe is important is, well, gosh, designed to be noticed as important (via color, font, size, etc.).

As someone who's striving to become a more effective communicator, you're constantly working on being more confident, more relaxed, more in charge...more 'you'. As you become more 'you' in presentation opportunities, you may be surprised to discover that you actually have a style of presenting, another description for you being you.

The concept of "you are your style" was made clear to me in art school during a painting class, as a teacher critiqued a student's painting.

"But, that's my style," the student said.

The teacher responded, without malice, "You're too young to have a style."

He was not being flippant or denigrating. He was conveying that style, in any creative endeavor, is a reflection of a person's core, a creatively delivered, exterior manifestation of what makes a person that particular person. The reason it takes years to actually 'have' a style is that it takes years to let go of everything we attempt to be, of how we attempt to portray ourselves, and simply be ourselves. The old adage of learning to be comfortable in our own skin is essentially saying we should just be ourselves, but it takes years to accept that it's okay to do just that.

This applies to you as a communicator, because the effective communicator's only agenda is to convey the truth, and the only way to convey the truth is to be true. Think of the movies you've seen, or the stories you've read, where a character's life finally comes together when he or she has the revelation that "this isn't who I really am..."

An example of this in a presentation environment is the communicator who does not have a natural ability to be funny, but believes that he should try to be funny to be effective.

Funny is difficult. Funny is damn hard. Saying things that are funny, telling jokes, and appreciating humor is one thing; having a natural gift for funny is something different entirely.

The same can be said of being really, really smart, not just street smart, college degree smart, or even did-damn-well-in-school smart, but rocket scientist, combination microbiologist and computer engineering PhD intelligent. Anyone who attempts to stand in front of an audience comprised of those really smart people and attempts to convey that they too are that kind of smart, when they're not, is a presentation disaster in the making.

I'm not conveying that you shouldn't be as funny as you can naturally be, or that you should assume that everyone is so much smarter than you – I'm conveying that an audience appreciates, and deserves, the real you.

Your style is you.

And you, as a style, will come through as you present content that you believe in.

You do that by connecting to the audience.

When you present data that you believe is truly, objectively remarkable, let your emotions come through in your tone of voice, or by your body language. In the example about the executive who never connected emotionally to a speech, the executive's attempt to 'look' concerned came off as frowning because the facial muscles weren't driven by genuine emotion.

It may not be physiologically accurate to state that it's the heart that controls our expressions, but it's closer to true than not.

With all the sincerity and passion flowing from you as you present, don't slip into tossed-off, self-denigration of yourself or content. It's subtle, and if you're thinking you wouldn't do that, or that you've never done that, ask yourself if during a presentation you've ever said, "This is just a slide that shows..."

It usually occurs when a presenter is concerned about staying on schedule, or wasn't confident about including the slide, left it in, and then decides it should have been cut. Regardless, if you're short on time, or you now regret leaving it in (and you're not using the Presenter View, so you can't easily skip ahead), don't say "this is just...", because you do have alternatives:

Advance past the slide and say, "I'm going to move forward to save some time."

Advance past the slide and don't mention why. Unless you were about to reveal some stunning, galactic secret, the audience won't put up a fuss or react. They have given themselves over to you for the length of the presentation. The only way things will upset them is if you indicate they will be or should be upset.

Show the slide and shorten what you had planned to say.

As you present something that affects you, excites you, enrages you, tickles you, don't ignore those feelings. Let your audience know when you're giving them something special, that warrants extra attention, that needs to taken away and shared with the rest of the world.

When you allow people to share your emotions, you are sharing your passion.

Time: your friend, your enemy

Don't lose track of it. Time is valuable; you don't want someone to waste yours, and you don't want to waste someone else's. It's an aspect within all the Performance attributes: awareness, content, empathy, focus.

Events run on a schedule, just as we run on a schedule. If something goes off schedule, everyone is affected.

Stay on time.

With few exceptions, the majority of presenters and speakers run long; this includes me, and I work hard to be better about it. It takes time and experience to work with the pacing of a live presentation situation. Controlled presentation time management begins early, in the presentation's development. It's where you grasp the interplay between what you've written, how you say what you've written, and how much time it really takes to say it. Rehearsing is the only way to properly experience how quickly each second goes by as you try to be concise, accurate, and somewhat engaging.

Einstein may have sorted out time and relativity, but the mysterious mechanics behind why a second feels like an hour for a presenter in front of an audience are still a mystery.

A misplaced note card, pages or slides out of order, even the pause to take a drink of water, can be perceived as taking an ungodly amount of time. It's our perception that gets us rattled, because even though a few seconds is not really that much time, when an unseen situation occurs – the system freeze that won't allow us to advance the slide – our awareness of a room filled with people waiting...waiting...still waiting...may push our panic button.

Stay calm and focused; recognize that something other than your presentation is happening; don't ignore it.

If your slide program freezes, don't keep clicking your laptop or wireless controller as you ignore your audience – try it a couple of times and then say, "Okay, while we wait for technology to catch up to us, let me describe what's on the next slide..." and then describe the slide.

If something at the back of the room falls to the floor with a huge clatter, don't keep speaking as if nothing happened, go ahead and say something like, "Everyone all right back there?"

There's an uncomfortable group feeling that spreads quickly when the only person in the room who acts as if nothing happened is the presenter. It's awkward and unnerving.

If an audience member insists on interrupting or asking a question before the presentation is finished (the third-worst case scenario), you need to respond in some fashion. You can say, "There will be a Q&A after the presentation", repeat it if necessary, and avoid carrying on a dialog. If it seems to be a tense situation, you need to stop and ask for security (second-worst case scenario).

(For the record, the worst-case scenario is when all hell breaks loose, which can be anything from a fire alarm to an earthquake. Stay as calm as possible, do what you have to do to stay safe, and forget about your presentation.)

The one-second-feels-like-an-hour phenomena also occurs when a speaker or presenter attempts to do something she hasn't attempted before. I once watched an executive director at an important press conference spend almost twenty seconds in an unsuccessful attempt to shorten a microphone stand for someone.

Whether it's adjusting a microphone stand, changing the position of a chair on stage (it's probably either taped down, or been placed in a specific position for the stage lighting or for a camera shot), or any other number of seemingly innocent alterations, don't put yourself in the position of experiencing that expanded time feeling; don't do it if you haven't done it before.

The audience – oh, the faces you will see, the things you will hear...

They are there because they are interested in what you have to say.

Could be they already agree with you; or disagree with you; or they're willing to give you an opportunity to convince them one way or the other. They might not have an opinion at all, and they're just curious.

They're your audience, whether three people, three hundred, or three thousand. The number objectively shouldn't matter to you...shouldn't being the caveat.

Meeting with three people to present yourself, reveal your research, or convert them from potential customer to buyer, is a very different environment than speaking to twenty, thirty, or more people for the same reason. Any attempt to convince you otherwise would be a disservice. How you physically and emotionally feel in a smaller, intimate environment is, at first, radically different than what you go through when you step in front of a much larger audience. The principles of connecting with an intimate or large audience are the same, but the ambient energy of the environment and its effect on you will be different.

As Journey was first rising to new heights of popularity, the band began to headline shows in outdoor stadiums. At the tour's first stadium show, where the crowd would number more than eighty-thousand, I overheard the stage manager advise singer Steve Perry during sound check to take a long look at the crowd later, just before the band actually took the stage for their set. It wasn't that Perry couldn't handle it, but our stage manager knew that Steve needed to see the enormity of the crowd before actually coming out to perform. The impact of eighty-thousand people, all focused on one person, can be psychologically overwhelming.

Good on ya' if you ever get an audience of eighty-thousand; most of us don't have to deal with those kinds of numbers. The point remains valid even when scaled down: it can be unnerving to present or speak for the first time to a large room filled with people.

Look into the audience, scan the faces, and find the people whose expressions are soft, pleasant, or happy. Each one of them is an oasis. If there are people you know in the audience, let your eyes find them as you glance up from your notes or script.

They represent, at least outwardly, a safe, welcoming, resting place for your eyes. You don't have to hold on them too long, just a few words of a sentence is enough, then look back at your notes. Your safe area, the place you can always look to without pressure or concern, is the back of the room. No one in the audience really ever knows who or what you're actually looking at;

what matters is that you are looking at 'them'.

Any time you scan an audience, you will see facial expressions that alarm, concern, or confuse you.

Your thoughts may go something like:

"Ohmigosh, that guy is texting..."

"Is she sleeping?"

"Hey, she's nodding in agreement."

"Wow, that guy looks pissed off."

After your presentation, when you review your performance, you'll realize you had those conscious thoughts, yet you continued speaking and presenting.

Pretty cool, huh? Your head took care of you.

Few of us have any idea of how we actually look as we listen to something. We 'think' we know, but we really don't have a clue.

I once overheard someone say, "But, I was really having a good time," when he was shown a photo of himself in a group of listeners; objectively, his expression was something between grump and cynic. The disconnect occurs because when we are captivated by something of interest, our facial muscles relax. I call this the neutral-subjective face: neutral, because it is the person's natural or common expression; subjective, because when relaxed, the facial structure itself may emphasize physical elements that convey to an observer a mood, emotion, or sense that isn't actually present. A naturally furrowed brow, prominent cheekbones, folds of skin, lifestyles, health, age, and personal issues all influence how people 'look'.

The audience member who momentarily rattles you because she seems so dissatisfied may actually be having a great time.

Conversing with your audience

Making eye-contact with people in the audience is only the start of a connection. Making and holding eye-contact as you say something, as if you're saying it to them, is the next step. When you begin to feel comfortable finding the oasis members of your audience, your next step is to find those that are ready to be part of a dialog. These are the audience members that subtly nod in agreement with you, or smile, perhaps chuckle at your humor.

They are the people you find and stay on as you ask and

answer your own question, but you allow them to share in the moment, silently answering you.

But don't put your audience, or a single audience member, in the spotlight, unless you have a good reason.

Jerry Seinfeld, Bill Cosby, and Ellen Degeneres are a few of the great comedians who during their acts regularly engage individuals in the audience. "You know what I mean, right?" as they point directly at someone. The audience is already primed to be a part of the act, many hoping to be; it's a different energy than situations most communicators encounter. That doesn't mean you can't have the same dialog with audience members, but it does mean you have to be much more discerning in how and when you choose to do it.

In most presentation environments, few people in the audience want to be the focus of attention; they are there to listen and observe, not to become part of the act.

The most common example of this is the lack of response to a question thrown out to the audience: "How many here have ever felt that way?...been to the Netherlands?...seen someone with blue hair?..."

"Anyone? Anyone out there?"

All of us have either been in an audience or watched as a speaker searched for anyone willing to answer, willing to raise their hand. I've seen this occur at all levels, from mediocre presenter to the best public speakers. Some in the audience will answer to themselves, but would rather undergo surgery without anesthetic than be looked at by a room of strangers.

Rather than ask a direct question of your audience, put yourself in a position of describing, rather than asking about, something. This is the key to the stand-up comic's "you know what I'm talking about, right?" Rework the setup:

"The market for this is different in different places, like Kansas, for example. I was there not too long ago, and I was surprised by..."

As you're sharing this with your audience, look for those oasis audience members. If you detect a facial 'response' – widening smile, mouthing agreement or nodding – hold your eye contact and, without physically pointing or specifically indicating them, say "do you know what I mean?", or something similar. You will almost always get some kind of response, because although you have engaged them, you have not put them in the crosshairs of attention.

Many presentations need a show of hands to reinforce a point or contribute to the presentation's effectiveness. It's fine to simply ask, or you can be slightly more congenial about it: "I'd like to know how many of you have gone through a similar situation." Look at the audience and raise your own hand. They'll know what to do.

There will be moments when you can sense *something*, when you feel that you're losing the audience; people are fidgeting in their seats, or a people are leaving the room.

Stay focused. It may be that some feel you're giving them too much information, or too little, or they're bored, or they don't like you...

Stay focused. Don't go into a psychological self-evaluation during your presentation (or after, frankly).

If you are running long, or you are concerned that you're not going to get to your most important points, make a decision to jump ahead; you can do this because you know your content. Tell your audience that you're going to move forward to save some time, but that you'll be available after the presentation if they wish to follow-up on anything.

If, for whatever reason, people are leaving before you're finished, there's really nothing you can do, and their reasons for leaving may have nothing to do with you or your presentation.

Stay focused.

Stay focused.

"Thank you and goodnight!"
You made it to the end. Everything worked...or maybe everything didn't...or things could've been so much better...

It's okay; you did it.

Post-performance will be nowhere near as nerve-wracking as

the performance, but you need to remain in communicator mode.

You will receive compliments. You will be asked for specifics, for contact information, all kinds of things. Be open, articulate, and informative. In the best case situation, there will be a line or group of questioners. Your challenge is to share yourself and your knowledge with everyone while remaining aware of your own and your questioners' time constraints. Questions that require more than two minutes of answers are best dealt with later – the usual follow-up means and methods – and the majority of people who are truly interested in follow-up will assume the same. At a couple of minutes into any discussion with one person, when there are still many people waiting to speak with you, you need to politely but earnestly present the following:

"I can talk about that, yes, but if you can either wait a few minutes, or give me your contact information, I want to make sure that I give everyone some time." Some will indeed accept and stand to the side, waiting until you are finished, and others will provide their contact information.

Gather your material and all of your equipment. the atmosphere can be jumbled and busy after your presentation, which makes the post-presentation idiot check as important as the pre-show check.

At your first opportunity, make notes about the experience. It doesn't have to be a detailed post-mortem, nor does it have to be an intensive, detailed review. You will know what elements felt right or wrong, where you stumbled, where it wasn't as smooth as you hoped. But don't focus solely on the rough spots. Note where it worked well, better than you had hoped, and what graphics, pictures or data got notable responses.

Look forward to the feedback of co-workers or 'friendlies'. They will have responses you weren't prepared for but, overall, you will discover that most of what you felt is accurate.

That last point is very important: trust yourself, your feelings and intuitions, because you'll always be more right than wrong.

Congratulations, whether you've recently presented something and used The Way to Communicate method to help, or whether you've taken the guidance to heart, and you can't wait to do your speech, make your sales call, report, or presentation. It's a gift to be able to help people, and if you've been helped by what you've discovered on these pages, you have allowed me to connect with you in a very special way.

Please share your communication experiences with me and other communicators on The Way to Communicate blog. The more we communicate the better communicators we all become.

We need to connect, and reconnect, in ways that have fallen out of favor. In business and life, in the workplace and on the sidewalks, we need to be able to look at each other, and be grateful for and respectful of our special, unique place on this planet. Our communication tools and capabilities are vast, yet nothing we can invent comes close to the meaning conveyed by a simple gesture, by the look of our eyes, or the tone of our voice.

We can touch and comfort and excite in ways unique to us as a species. History is filled with pivotal moments in humanity that turned on a moment of personal connection, of how one person so moved another that society, culture, and lives were forever altered.

We all have the capacity to make special connections, to connect our shared humanity. My hope is that through The Way to Communicate, you will discover how it feels to connect with someone at their deepest, purest level.

When that happens, you will truly understand the way to communicate.

###

Afterword - Be True

It's a simple premise – Be True.

It's one of life's greatest challenges, virtually impossible to do in totality, but vitally important to attempt.

To Be True is to do, to live, to achieve, or to help, without agenda or motive for anything other than the 'doing' itself. It is a pure approach, akin to the Buddhist traits of living a pure life and having compassion and forgiveness for all, but it is an approach to life that transcends all philosophies. It's right up there with the Golden Rule: always treat others as you wish to be treated.

It's just the best way to live.

A box of Truth

Cracker Jack, as a brand and product, is still readily available, but isn't quite as well known as it was a few generations ago, when the actual "candy coated popcorn, peanuts…" that was the product was trumped by the "…and a prize" inside. The prizes then, in concept, were very much what they are now: small, usually paper-based, something that barely cost the company pennies to include in every box, but with an invaluable return-on-investment in brand awareness.

The prize is still delivered to the consumer as it has been for decades, inside an approximately two-inch square, sealed envelope, nestled amidst the popcorn and peanuts. Printed on each small envelope is fortune-cookie styled advice. At some point in my life, upon opening a box and pulling out the prize, I read words that formed a parable to live by: "Always tell the truth, and you'll never have to remember anything." It was most definitely not the exclusive copyright of Cracker Jack, and I have since seen it in different forms, in different venues.

I have no idea of its provenance, but it doesn't matter.

While the phrase is not as notable as other well-known sayings and quotes, it should be neither dismissed nor undervalued. The phrase, if one chooses to really parse it, may not be accurate for all people or situations, but as a general rule it conveys a simple, powerful truth, literally and figuratively.

If you are asked a question about something you've done, something you might or will do, and why you did, might or will do what you did or might do, and the motivations for your thoughts or actions were sincere – without malice, without lies, without hidden agenda – your answers can only be the truth. Your answers for why, how, etc., will be the same, in essence, as your actions.

If you lied, maneuvered, went around someone, stabbed someone in the back, inflated the figures, hid the facts, purposely misplaced the file, misdirected, obfuscated, or acted in some way to benefit yourself at the expense of someone or something, you'll have two ways to respond to the whys and hows: tell the truth or lie.

The truth never has to be 'remembered', because honest actions and honest reasons are, essentially, the same. The truth is what it is, while the particulars of a lie always have to be remembered. If the particulars of a lie are shuffled, altered, or simply forgotten, the lie becomes apparent, and everything that had been constructed upon the foundation of the lie begins to shift, falter, or fall.

I wrote about passion earlier, noting that passion is best expressed when it is 'allowed' to flow, when it is the result of the excitement about and the belief in something. The energy created by your unfettered belief in an idea or message is passion's propellant.

Living by the Be True philosophy clears the way for your passion's own "Houston, we have lift off".

Be True as a Communicator

Many of us know bullshit when we see or hear it. We're occasionally fooled, misled, mistaken, or simply taken in, but we learn from it, steam about it for a while and then move on. We keep that experience at hand and use it as a measure, an indicator whenever we begin to doubt something, feel uncomfortable about it, or just sense that "something here ain't right."

Occasionally, we'll be mistaken. Sometimes it's our fault, our bad, for whatever reason.

But there are times we go directly to our internal BS meter due to the way something was presented to us; how it was presented to us; or because the presenter, the communicator, spoke or behaved in a way that put us off, made us doubt or refuse to connect.

It's a sad truth, but there are poor communicators who have pure hearts, sincere motivations, and an important message to be communicated, and it's all for naught, because we won't let them in. We won't give ourselves up. The communicator may be sloppy in appearance, or the presentation materials may be confusing or hard to fathom. Perhaps he was late and never got into his rhythm; perhaps her tone is caustic, sharp, or disdainful; maybe she never looked at the audience.

Those are ways that not being true in the present undermines a communicator. But for many of us it is in the way we are true, or not, on a daily basis that presents the greater challenge to future communication situations.

Throughout the previous pages, I presented scenarios, insights, and guidance on using the attributes of awareness and empathy in everyday situations, whether during a brief conversation as you walk into your company's building, or introducing yourself at a social event. If you are true in these interactions, and in all your motivations, actions and reactions, you will carry and convey that truth as a communicator no matter what you are doing. You will dress respectfully for your audience, because you always dress appropriately. Your presentation materials will always facilitate the delivery of your message, not distract from it, because that's how your materials are always designed. And you will connect with your audience, because you strive to connect with everyone, always, whether to friend, to co-worker, or to seminar attendees.

The concept is simple – the execution takes effort.

At the beginning of this book, I introduced you to the

concept of knowing your end before you begin. This applies to understanding how Being True in the beginning sets you up to achieve your optimal moment of communication in the future, where you are most effective being 'you'.

Envision two communicators: one strives to Be True; the other does whatever is necessary to move through life, even if it is at the expense of others.

One takes the time to communicate, to inquire, to study, to engage with people, to find common ground, to listen with all her senses, to convey that which is true, that she cares. She finds an extra minute when someone needs one from her; in return, she finds that people listen to her, welcome her, pay attention to and absorb her message. They know that she is the same person they know one-to-one as she is when leading the team, running the meetings, setting the goals.

The other communicator, someone in the same position, gives or withholds time based on whether he benefits or not. His conversations are self-centered, and while his team gets the job done, makes its numbers, achieves its goals, no one on his team feels as if they are part of the success – they feel as though they are the unseen, unappreciated drivers of that for which he takes full credit. His presentations are accurate but tiring, and his message may be received, but is also remembered as "nothing special."

At some point, at a meeting where both communicators have something at stake and must compete for the hearts and minds of all, only one communicator will have already connected with many in the audience simply by entering the room.

That communicator is who you should strive to be, and you can; be true.

To Be True:
"I'll be there at three." Be there at three.

"This will take up some personal time, but it's really important to us." Make it important to you too.

There's Nick, who's going through a tough time. "Nick, what can I do for you?"

How you look and behave at the event tonight will reflect directly on the company. Dress and comport yourself as if you

ARE the company.

For all those decisions and commitments made to yourself, where no one but you will know if you have a cigarette even though you're trying to quit; eat a snack while you're dieting; told yourself you'd be in the office early; committed to attending a party but are striving to find a way out of it...commit to Be True to yourself, and do the true thing.

Here are the realities: the world at large, and the individual worlds we live in, make it close to impossible to Be True at every moment. We are not perfect, nor should we wish we were. We do what we must to survive, and we do what we must to make the best lives for ourselves and our families. Occasionally, we must deliver the kick in the crotch or the sucker punch. Occasionally, we must tap into our base emotions and let our anger and volume rise. We can't always prevent the slip of the tongue, something said or done in haste, and we will not find it in ourselves to love everyone with whom we meet, nor respect those that we know we should, but just can't bear the thought of it.

We will not always get the rewards or recognition we deserve.

Occasionally, the bastards will win.

But, never capitulate. Never stop being true. Never allow yourself to be pushed off what you know is the correct path.

Gains achieved by deceit are like friendships formed through lies: they will not last.

Be true.

Just be true.

Acknowledgments

I have been influenced, guided, loved and liked by many wonderful people. To my own consternation, I have not always communicated to them just how much I appreciate their friendship, support, and wise counsel. Here, then, is an effort to convey my thanks and appreciation.

Mom and dad, for everything. Moe, for our shared souls. Marion, Ken, and Laura, for extended family. Bill and Linda Lee, for family, support, and fun. Tom and Mary, for help with the house. Lou Naidorf, for a special relationship. Steph Adams, for being the best, and hanging around for twenty-six years. Susan Barnes, for closeness and partnership. Bob Cetera, for saving my life in high school. My Schwinn Moab, for saving my life in 2001. Bob Spryszak, for lasting friendship, and for saving my life last year. Camie Foust, for love and creative growth. Allen Fish, for expanding my horizons. Richard Ruggieri, for letting me in. Maureen Merrill, for partnership and work. Mark Osmun, for bringing me in. Lorraine Evanoff, for still reading. Gregg Bagni, for still being here. Barry Schienberg, for your uncompromising principals. Norm Rosinski, for the chance to participate and for the steady work.

Patrick Kriwanek, for early mentoring. Richard Hymns, for the room, and for letting me hold the Oscar. Mick Anger, for your vision. Jacky Andrews, for the opportunity to grow and learn. Alice Boylan, for unwavering support. Peter Fitzgerald, for your Mac II. Pat Morrow, for opening the door. Terry "Gonzo" Brennan, for the laughs and secrets. Neal, Ross, Steve, Steve, Jonathan, Greg, and Aynsley, for showing me the universe. Benny, Chris, and Sal, for allowing me to see the view from the summit for a couple of months. Benny and Audrey, and Flo, for your early support (I haven't forgotten). That screenwriter across the canyon from me in Mill Valley, for 'making' me write my first screenplay in 1982 and then pointing out all the things that were wrong with it. Richard Gladstein, for graciously giving me twenty-five minutes.

Elizabeth, because I'd be nothing without you.

To access additional content and information on
Way to Communicate seminars, go to
www.thewaytocommunicate.com

www.ingramcontent.com/pod-product-compliance
Lightning Source LLC
Chambersburg PA
CBHW060119050426
42448CB00010B/1947